THE
PLANTAGENETS

THE PLANTAGENETS

A HISTORY OF ENGLAND'S BLOODIEST DYNASTY, FROM HENRY II TO RICHARD III, 1154 – 1485

BEN HUBBARD

amber
BOOKS

Published by
Amber Books Ltd
United House
North Road
London N7 9DP
United Kingdom
www.amberbooks.co.uk
Instagram: amberbooksltd
Facebook: www.facebook.com/amberbooks
Twitter: @amberbooks

ISBN: 978-1-78274-649-2

Project Editor: Sarah Uttridge
Designer: Hart McLeod Ltd.
Picture Research: Terry Forshaw

Printed in China

Contents

INTRODUCTION

According to legend, the Plantagenet royal line was literally the devil's spawn. Their ancestor was the Count of Anjou, whose beautiful bride refused to attend mass. Confronted, she revealed herself as a devil and flew from the highest church window. All 15 Plantagenet kings were said to carry her demonic blood.

THIS COUNTESS of Anjou was alleged to be a daughter of Satan, or perhaps the serpent-fairy of medieval folklore, Melusine. One of the four sons she bore, was 'Fulk the Black', a notorious murderer and rapist who burned his wife at the stake in her wedding dress. Many believed the Plantagenets inherited their ferocious temper from Fulk; their golden-red hair came from Geoffrey the Handsome (1113–51), the future Count of Anjou and founder of the Plantagenet family line.

The French county of Anjou was the homeland of the Plantagenets, although few of its kings actually bore that name. Instead, it derived from the yellow broom plant, *planta genista*, a sprig of which was worn by Geoffrey on his hat. Geoffrey owned extensive territories in France, but did not rule, nor take any interest in England. That was instead the domain of his bride, Empress Matilda, widow of the Holy Roman Emperor and granddaughter of William the Conqueror.

Opposite: A representation of the enamel effigy of Geoffrey V, Count of Anjou, on his tomb at Le Mans Cathedral.

Above: The Great Seal of the Empress Matilda, heir to Henry I and wife of Geoffrey of Anjou.

Below: A mock fight between cousins Matilda and Stephen, who both vied for the English crown.

Matilda was notoriously haughty and headstrong, and she wore her various titles with an arrogant pride. She therefore took it as a grave insult when her father, King Henry I of England, suggested she married Geoffrey of Anjou. Matilda's last husband had been the Holy Roman Emperor, King Henry V of Germany, a powerful ruler who controlled a vast domain. Anjou, by comparison, was paltry, its heir a 15-year-old teenager. Matilda was 26 and a grand noblewoman in her prime.

Matilda, however, had no choice. Henry I did not have a male heir and hoped that Matilda's marriage would supply a male to become the future Count of Anjou and King of England. In the meantime, Henry made Matilda his heir, a rare occurrence in an age when the line of succession was from father to son.

Many of the barons of England refused to accept the rule of a queen, and when Henry died in 1135 they invited Matilda's cousin Stephen to seize the English throne. When Stephen did so it sparked a two-decade civil war known simply as 'the Anarchy'.

During the Anarchy, the English barons fell in behind either Stephen or Matilda, and long periods of attritional warfare followed. To bolster his support, Stephen invited foreign mercenaries to England who, once there, committed brutal atrocities. It was during this dark period that 'Christ and his saints slept' according to the Peterborough Chronicle, a 12th-century Anglo-Saxon text.

'They [the barons] sorely burdened the unhappy people of the country with forced labour on the castles; and when the castles were built, they filled them with devils and wicked men. By night and by day they seized those whom they believed to have any wealth, whether they were men or women; and in order to get their gold and silver, they put them into prison and tortured them with unspeakable tortures, for never were martyrs tortured as they were.'

– THE PETERBOROUGH CHRONICLE

The Peterborough Chronicle reported that the torturers hung people by their feet and smoked them over fires, or strung them up by the thumbs with chain mail armour strapped to their feet. Some had knotted cords tied to their heads, which were twisted until they broke through the skull; others were crushed in a shallow chest filled with sharp stones and stamped on; more still were simply thrown into dungeon oubliettes full of snakes, but with no food or water.

The war seemed to be about to end in 1142 when Stephen trapped Matilda in her castle in Oxford. His army laid siege for several months, and food inside grew perilously scarce. It was then, just before Christmas, that Matilda made a daring night-time escape dressed in a white cloak to camouflage herself against the snow. Her garrison surrendered the next day, but the deadlock of the Anarchy continued.

In the end, it took a male heir to resolve the English war of succession. This was Matilda and Geoffrey's eldest son, the future Henry II, one of England's most famous kings. Henry had all the characteristics typical of a Plantagenet: red-gold hair, a fiery temper and an insatiable desire to extend his power and lands.

Among Henry's successors were the infamous English kings known so well to history: Richard the Lionheart, the Evil King John, and the nephew-murdering Richard III. Internecine murder and warfare is a hallmark of the Plantagenet story.

Above: Here, Matilda performs her daring escape from Oxford Castle during the dead of night.

Henry II's sons famously declared war on their father and nearly killed him with an arrow when he came to talk terms. As he handed over his kingdom to Richard, Henry snarled that he wished God would give him enough life to get revenge on his son.

Henry died a broken man, but he was one of the few Plantagenets to die of natural causes. Nor did many die a hero's death on the battlefield. Dysentery was the leading killer, of kings as well as of common people. The most devastating medieval sickness was the 14th-century Black Death, which killed more than a quarter of the population; it took King Edward III's daughters too.

Below: The Royal Arms of England, shown here, were first adopted in the 12th century by the Plantagenet kings.

Edward was the romantic warrior king who fostered a national love of Arthurian legend and with it the ideals of chivalry. Edward held lavish tournaments known as Round Tables and led his army into war against the French. At Crécy, Edward wrought terrible devastation upon his enemy using thousands of archers with longbows; this new military tactic made the English army and its banner of St George the most feared in Europe.

St George and the three golden lions were only two of many symbols developed for the English kingdom under the Plantagenets. During their rule the Plantagenets transformed the cultural and political landscape of England: they built grand castles and gothic cathedrals, created the country's parliament and its systems of justice, and made English, rather than French or Latin, the official language of government.

Right: Many of the Plantagenets' great castles remain standing today. Dover Castle, constructed by Henry II, is England's largest.

However, these constitutional legacies don't account for the dark appeal and lasting infamy of the Plantagenets. Rather it is their irresistible dynastic saga of murder, madness, betrayal and civil war. Few of the Plantagenet monarchs were good kings or decent men; but they are memorable monsters. Consider the catalogue of crimes and atrocities that occurred between the 12th-century Anarchy and the 1485 slaying of Richard III that ended the Plantagenet line.

These include: the murder of archbishop Thomas Becket by Henry II's knights in Canterbury Cathedral; the 25-year squabble between Henry III and Simon de Montfort that resulted in the gruesome defilement of the knight's body; the obsessional love between Edward II and Piers Gaveston that ended in the king's alleged demise by hot poker; and the tyranny of Richard II leading to the Wars of the Roses, the most poetically named of England's national bloodbaths.

The Wars of the Roses brought the Plantagenets full circle: their dynastic reign began during civil war and it would end during another. The end was as brutal as the beginning; it was perhaps a fitting conclusion. 'From the devil we sprang and to the devil we shall go,' Richard the Lionheart loved to say. This is the story of his family, the Plantagenets, the royal dynasty born of the demon Countess of Anjou.

Below: The royal standard is laid at the altar at St Paul's Cathedral following the Battle of Bosworth Field. Richard III, the last Plantagenet king, was killed during this battle.

1

HENRY II

King Henry II is best remembered for the bloody murder of Thomas Becket, the Archbishop of Canterbury. By chance or mishap, Henry infamously caused four knights to slaughter the priest in Canterbury Cathedral by crying: 'Will no one rid me of this turbulent priest?'

T HE FIRST Plantagenet king never actually uttered the sentence about the 'turbulent priest'. However, at the time, Henry was angry, drunk and tired after a long evening of feasting. What he actually said, moreover, was threatening enough. 'What miserable drones and traitors have I nurtured and promoted in my household,' he supposedly bellowed, 'who let their lord be treated with such shameful contempt by a low-born cleric?'

Becket was indeed not of noble blood, but rather the son of a London merchant whose star was on the wane after a meteoric ascent through Henry's court to the highest religious office of the land. Not that any of this mattered to the four knights who sat earnestly through Henry's tirade and concluded it to be a direct order from their sovereign. They immediately set out at a hard

Opposite: Archbishop of Canterbury Thomas Becket is confronted by the four knights who famously took his life in the cathedral.

gallop from Henry's court in Bures, Normandy, to Canterbury and reached the cathedral a few days later.

Becket was in his inner chambers at dusk on 29 December 1170, when the heavily armed knights burst through his door. An argument broke out and Becket retreated, hurrying away to hear vespers. Now angry, the knights followed Becket into the cathedral and attempted to drag him outside. Becket resisted, crying out that if they wished violence upon him they would

Right: Henry II had inherited both the Plantagenet golden-red hair and the fiery temperament: his tantrums were legendary.

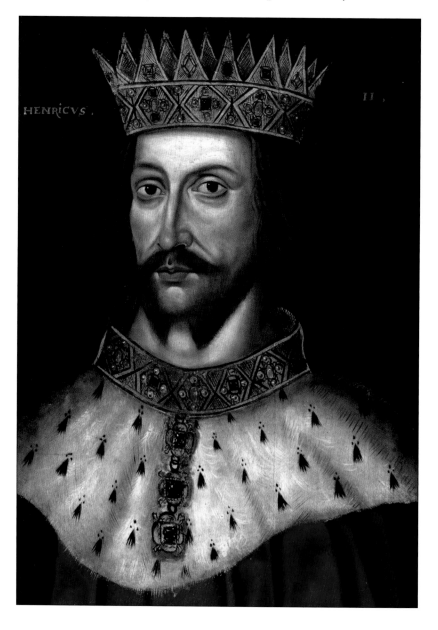

have to carry it out there, on consecrated ground. He grabbed a nearby pillar and held on for his life.

Swords were then drawn and Becket was struck with the flat of one knight's sword. 'Fly! You are a dead man,' he told Becket as another dealt him a blow on his head. Blood streamed down Becket's face and he fell to his knees. Another knight then swung at Becket with such force that he cut off the top of his skull and shattered his blade against the stone floor. The others proceeded to butcher Becket where he lay, one using his sword point to spread around the Archbishop's brains. He then called out to his comrades: 'Let us away, knights; he will rise no more.'

Standing in stunned silence in the shadows of the cathedral were Becket's ecclesiastical staff. These were the men who would report the atrocity to the horrified ears of European Christendom. None were excluded from the appalled condemnation of Henry that followed. Louis VII of France, who had earlier lost his bride Eleanor to Henry and hated him passionately, demanded 'unprecedented retribution'. 'Let the sword of Saint Peter unleashed to avenge the martyr of Canterbury,' Louis wrote.

It would take three years for Becket to be canonized, but in the meantime his martyrdom was an instantaneous scandal. The people of Canterbury rushed to the murder scene waving pieces of cloth that they dipped in his blood and then tasted, and in some cases, put into their eyes. Sensing the possibilities, the priests of Canterbury immediately struck up a thriving trade in Becket's blood. It was gathered and mixed as a tincture, heavily diluted with water, and sold in small, custom-made alloy vessels with the inscription

Below: The Becket Casket is a 12th-century gilt-copper and champlevé enamel reliquary depicting the murder of the Archbishop. Its contents are no longer present.

Above: This badge of Thomas Becket's head was a common souvenir sold to pilgrims visiting his shrine at Canterbury Cathedral. The badge proved that the pilgrim had made the journey and was said to heal the sick or dying.

'All weakness and pain is removed, the healed man eats and drinks, and evil and death pass away.'

For those not able to afford a vial of Becket water, brooches and pins depicting the Archbishop's likeness also became available. A kind of cult of Becket was created and pilgrims with mysterious ailments including cankerous sores and swollen limbs made long pilgrimages to his tomb. Chaucer's *The Canterbury Tales* is based on these pilgrims. Any member of the unwell who did not receive a healing miracle via the dead Becket was simply told they lacked the inherent faith to begin with. Nothing would slow the multitudes of pilgrims or the publicity it generated for Becket's martyrdom; news of his murder spread quickly.

The irony was that Henry seemed as shocked by the news of Becket's death as everyone else. After all, they had once been favourite friends. But more than that, Henry understood exactly what the fallout from the murder would entail: it would leave him as a pariah. He took to his bed for three days and refused food or water. He then set off for the furthest corner of Western Europe where he could stay out of view: Ireland.

THE KING'S BEGINNING

The Kingship of England had been one trial after another from the moment Henry, Duke of Normandy and Count of Anjou, took the throne at 21. Henry inherited his father Geoffrey of Anjou's golden-red hair and a propensity for violent and vindictive rages. During one such fit, Henry 'flung down his cap, undid his belt, threw from him his cloak and robes, tore the silk covering off his couch, and, sitting down as if on a dunghill, began to chew stalks of straw.'

Volatile and unpredictable anger was the characteristic that united all of the Plantagenet kings. On the one hand, Henry could be charming and held the wit and courtly courtesy expected of a medieval royal; he also dressed like a huntsman and was quick to take violent offence if he believed his authority undermined.

Henry was ruthlessly ambitious and his mother Matilda had urged him from boyhood to seize his birthright of England.

DESCRIBING THE KING

A CONTEMPORARY DESCRIPTION OF **Henry** comes from the Archdeacon of Brecon and historian Gerald of Wales, who wrote an account of the king's 1171 conquest of Ireland. Although something of a panegyric, it does confirm other accounts of the king's vigour and his apparent inability to sit still.

'Henry II, King of England, was a man of reddish, freckled complexion with a large round head, grey eyes which glowed fiercely and grew bloodshot in anger, a fiery countenance and a harsh, cracked voice. His neck was somewhat thrust forward from his shoulders, his chest was broad and squat, his arms strong and powerful...He was addicted to chase beyond measure;

at crack of dawn he was off on horseback, traversing aster lands, penetrating forests and climbing the mountain tops, and so he passed restless days. At evening on his return home was rarely seen to sit down either before or after supper. After such wearisome exertions he would wear out the whole court by continual standing.'

– *Expugnatio Hibernica*, Gerald of Wales

In his wife, Eleanor of Aquitaine, Henry had met an equal in ambition: the union brought great wealth to both parties and was also one of the great royal scandals of the age.

The traditional role of princesses during the Middle Ages was to be married off as a way of brokering an alliance between two great households. This could increase the wealth and assets of both or otherwise heal a rift that had previously resulted in conflict. Eleanor, however, was a rare combination of a keen brain and captivating beauty; medieval students in ale houses often sang bawdy songs about bedding her. Eleanor's lands of Aquitaine, which covered a vast swathe of western France, were prize enough in themselves for any royal suitor. Eleanor was, in short, the greatest catch of the 12th century.

Above: The Great Seal of King Henry II shows the king on his throne and astride his horse. Henry's passion for riding made him bowlegged over time.

King Louis VII of France wasted no time in marrying Eleanor himself, but the union was to be a disappointment for both newly-weds. Eleanor bore Louis two daughters but was unable to produce a needed male heir. Besides, Eleanor was a feisty, extravagant queen who loved luxury. Louis, by comparison, dressed drably and stuck to a simple diet. Eleanor once remarked: 'I've married a monk, not a monarch!' In the end, it was Eleanor who sought an annulment from Louis. To add insult to this injury, Eleanor was soon riding to the bedside of her next betrothed: Henry. The journey was dangerous, as several nobles had set out to kidnap Eleanor and force her into marriage, so desirable was her hand.

Eleanor's marriage to Henry brought experience and sophistication to match the Plantagenet brawn: Eleanor was 30, Henry 19, and both wanted the world. With their territories combined and the lands later conquered by Henry, the couple would rule over a kingdom that stretched from Scotland to the Pyrenees; it represented the height of the Plantagenet's physical dominion. Eleanor's ambition, however, would prove to be Henry's undoing.

> VOLATILE AND UNPREDICTABLE ANGER WAS THE CHARACTERISTIC THAT UNITED ALL OF THE PLANTAGENET KINGS.

Right: Henry II and Eleanor are depicted riding into Winchester on their way to the king's coronation in London.

Nevertheless, when Henry landed on the shores of England to claim the English throne and quell the civil war that had wracked the country for 16 years, it must have been a comfort to know Eleanor was standing steadfast beside him. England at that time was not a particularly desirable proposition. Henry landed at Malmesbury in Wiltshire, a town loyal to his enemy, King Stephen, with a small army numbering around 3000 infantry and 150 knights.

Henry's winter crossing of the English Channel had been tempestuous, and he marched towards Malmesbury in a filthy mood. The castle itself was half-ruined after three years of siege. Inside, the exhausted inhabitants prepared, once again, to defend their town as Henry planned how to destroy it. The *Gesta Stephani*, a history of King Stephen, recounts the action:

Above: This map shows the extent of the Plantagenet kingdom directly after Henry II took the English crown.

'So the Duke [Henry] collecting his forces, and with the barons flocking in eagerly to join him, made without delay for the castle of Malmesbury, which was subject to the king, and when a crowd of common people flew to the wall surrounding the town as through to defend it he ordered the infantry, men of the greatest cruelty, which he brought with him, some to assail the defenders with arrows and missiles, others to devote all their efforts to demolishing the wall.

When the town of Malmesbury was captured…behold, not long afterwards the king [Stephen] arrived with a countless army collected from all his supporters everywhere, as though he meant to fight a pitched battle with the duke, as the armies of both sides stood in array with a river dividing them it was arranged between them and carefully settled that they should demolish the castle, both because they could not join battle on account of the river and its very deep valley intervening and because it was a bitter winter with a severe famine in those parts.'

— GESTA STEPHANI

Severe famine, civil war, a bitter winter. It's a bleak picture of a broken England, a state torn and rudderless, desperate to be reconciled and reunited. Understanding this, Henry employed diplomacy rather than bloodshed to bring the English to his side. First he sent his mercenaries home – the English loathed the foreign fighters who had robbed, harassed and murdered so many during the Anarchy. Next he invited Stephen to parley. This was done more out of necessity than guile: expecting Henry's attack to come at Wallingford Castle rather than Malmesbury, Stephen had led his army on a forced march for the 80km (50 miles) between the two.

By the time Stephen reached Malmesbury his army was drenched and harried by a biting wind. Many could not hold their dripping wet lances. They outnumbered Henry's men, but

Below: An illustration depicting the meeting between Henry and Stephen across the River Thames. Their deal saw Henry crowned King of England less than a year later.

none had the stomach for a fight. The civil war had all but burnt itself out. In the end Stephen agreed to negotiate with Henry. Their agreement, called the Treaty of Winchester, promised that Henry could become King of England, as was his birthright, but only after Stephen had died. This turned out to be providential, as less than a year later Stephen complained of 'a violent pain in his gut accompanied by a flow of blood' and collapsed shortly afterwards. Henry was crowned at Westminster Abbey alongside Eleanor on 19 December 1154.

KING HENRY

King Henry II still had a lot to do in England. Under Stephen, many castles, towns and land had been given away to foreign lords in return for support of arms. Henry ordered the expulsion of all foreign mercenaries who had benefited from these favours, in particular the hated Flemish. He then began to demolish the many illegal castles that had sprung up during the Anarchy. Next, Henry went head to head with other barons plotting rebellion.

The most notable of these was Hugh de Mortimer, owner of four castles including Wigmore, who refused to swear fealty to Henry. The king marched his army to Wigmore, but in another display of diplomatic finesse, declined to give the order to attack.

Below: The remains of Wigmore Castle, stronghold of rebel baron Hugh de Mortimer. Mortimer would proclaim his loyalty to Henry without a drop of blood being spilled.

Instead Henry paused just long enough outside the castle for a panicked Hugh to wave the white flag. Even then, Henry did not punish the baron. Instead he rode his army into the castle and straight back out again. Henry was sending a clear message to Hugh and any other baron contemplating treason: he was the king and in England his control was absolute.

IN HIS REFORMS HENRY UNWITTINGLY INSTITUTED A LEGAL SYSTEM THAT TODAY FORMS THE BASIS FOR LAW IN BOTH BRITAIN AND THE UNITED STATES.

Shows of force were a useful temporary measure; a more systematic strategy was needed to create lasting stability. Henry had to find a way of both humouring and taming the barons. To do this he assembled an entirely new type of army: one made up of law clerks. Law would become Henry's weapon of centralized control, and he would administer it by means of travelling judges in each of England's counties. Up until then justice had been the domain of the sheriffs. English law itself was a hotchpotch of rules introduced by the Normans to oppress the English alongside the more ancient customs enacted by the Anglo-Saxons.

To dispense Henry's justice, travelling judges, known as 'assizes', would arrive in a town or village, proceed down the high street with the sheriff and other dignitaries in tow, and then sit at a local hall to overhear a case. The judges would return to their headquarters at London's Westminster Hall and compare notes with colleagues who had been administering justice in other parts of the realm. These discussions and the punishments served for crimes laid out a common set of principles, or precedents, which aimed to ensure consistency in the administration of justice. In time this became known as common law.

One of the responsibilities of the judges was to resolve disputes over land. This was a common problem in 12th-century Britain, a rural society whose central interest lay in dominion over arable land. For these cases, the judges would instruct 12 men to help them with the case and offer advice – a jury. Trial by jury thereafter replaced trial by battle and trial by ordeal, the previous means of settling disputes. In his reforms Henry unwittingly instituted a legal system that formed the basis for law still used today in both Britain and the United States.

TYPES OF TRIALS

TRIALS BY ORDEAL AND battle were legal methods, introduced by Anglo-Saxons, which left it to God to determine a person's guilt or innocence. Ordeals were normally used when no other evidence, such as eye-witness accounts, was available. There were three such trials: by hot water or hot iron, by cold water, and by consecrated bread. All were administered by a priest in a church before witnesses.

In a trial by hot water, the accused was invited to pick up a stone from the bottom of cauldron of boiling water. In a trial by hot iron, the accused was asked to carry a red-hot piece of iron across a specified distance. In both cases, the accused was considered innocent if after three days God had healed the wounds rather than let them fester.

In a trial by cold water, the accused had their feet and hands bound and were then thrown in a river, pond or sanctified water. If the accused floated they would be declared guilty; if they sank, innocent. The rather more benign trial by consecrated bread was a

way of testing the innocence of a cleric. The accused would be asked to swallow a piece of bread, and, if it made them choke, God was showing them to be guilty.

The Normans' usual method of resolving a dispute over land or money was trial by battle, a duel between the two parties with the winner said to be the one favoured by God. The loser of the battle, if still alive, would often then be executed as punishment.

Right: Villagers carry out a trial by cold water. The trial seldom ended well for the accused.

None of Henry's legal reforms were enacted for the common good of his ordinary subjects. They were created simply to control the populace and fill the king's coffers. Fines and other payments for breaking the law went straight to Henry; barons and other wealthy men were expected to give the king a monetary gift to grease the judicial cogs. In his legal reforms, therefore, Henry had successfully placed his barons under the royal thumb while also turning a healthy profit. However, his judicial reform could not reach the institution that had long been a rival for power with European monarchs: the Church.

In the 12th century, nearly one in six Englishmen belonged to the clergy. Many were poor, badly educated and even illiterate, but all enjoyed protection under the Church against criminal punishment. Clergymen, in other words, who stole, raped, maimed or killed, would receive their sentence from the Church's own papal court – and the Church had a well-founded reputation for lenient treatment of its own. The exemption of clergymen from his new laws enraged the king; he regarded it as an insult to his regal authority. The Church would have to be dealt with.

Right: A 12th-century depiction of prisoners awaiting trial in stocks and tethers.

An opportunity presented itself in 1161, with the death of Theobald the Archbishop of Canterbury. To bridge the gap between Crown and Church, Henry could install his own candidate. This was of course his friend and chancellor and the man he would later murder: Thomas Becket.

BROTHERS IN BLOOD

Becket impressed Henry from the moment they met. He was a clerk for Archbishop Theobald, and Henry was immediately struck by his confident and pragmatic approach. The two became famous friends, hunting partners and drinking companions. Before long, Henry had made Becket his chancellor.

Below: Thomas Becket is shown in conversation with Henry II in Peter Langtoft's 13th-century *Chronicle*, a history of England.

It was a match of opposites: Becket was tall, dark-haired and pale with a long nose who, despite being of common stock, styled himself as a wealthy nobleman of importance. His patrician style was the perfect foil for the squat, ruddy king, who hated pageantry and courtly ceremony, and indeed, anything that might confine him to sitting still.

Henry teased Becket about his fine clothes. Once, when riding through the snow-covered streets of London, Henry remarked that it would be a charitable thing to give a nearby shivering beggar a warm cloak. When Becket agreed that it would, Henry tore the cape from his chancellor's back and threw it to the beggar. Henry took pleasure in irritating the pompous Becket; he would ride his horse into Becket's dining hall before leaping from the saddle to eat. However, Henry was also pleased to leave his chancellor in charge of court pageantry, at which Becket excelled.

THE PARIS TRAIN

BECKET's biographer and travelling companion William Fitzstephen describes one of the Chancellor's trips to Paris. For such excursions, Becket travelled with a train of pack horses, carts and servants and brought gifts of jewellery, clothes and even monkeys to King Louis VII. Designed to dazzle all who witnessed the procession, such trips were publicity stunts paid for by Henry and executed by Becket:

'Eight wagons conveyed all the requisites for the journey, drawn by five high-bred horses; at the head of each horse was a groom on foot, "dressed in a new tunic."…The Chancellor's chapel-furniture had its own wagon, his chamber had one, his pantry another, his kitchen another; others carried provisions, and others again the baggage of the party; amongst them, twenty-four suits of clothing for presents, as well as furs and carpets. Then there were twelve sumpter-horses; eight chests containing the Chancellor's gold and silver plate; and besides a very considerable store of coin, "some books" found room…two hundred and fifty young Englishmen led the way in knots of six or ten or more together, singing their national songs as they entered the French villages…lastly came the Chancellor himself, surrounded by his intimate friends. "What must the King of England be," said the French as he went by, "if his Chancellor travels in such state?"'

– *THE LIFE AND MARTYRDOM OF SAINT THOMAS BECKET*, WILLIAM FITZSTEPHEN

Left: Thomas Becket is shown at the head of his ostentatious train as it makes its way through France towards Paris.

With his interest in ostentatious displays of power and material wealth, it is perhaps understandable that many of England's clerics found Becket a poor fit for the job of Archbishop of Canterbury. He wasn't exactly monastic in his approach. There were other objections to the appointment: Becket's academic record was poor, he was too close to the king, he appeared by all accounts to be a secular figure, and had previously been verbally abusive to the monks while working for Theobald. Even Becket was unsure about his own credentials. He was, however, an ambitious man who did nothing by halves. If the king wanted him to be the archbishop, then he would be the archbishop, and he would make it his life's work.

Above: Thomas Becket is here immortalized in the middle stained glass window at St David's Cathedral, Wales.

Becket's religious detractors shouldn't have worried, for when Henry made him archbishop, he embraced his new role with a passionate fanaticism. First, Becket resigned as chancellor as he felt the two roles to clearly be at odds with each other. With the chancellorship went the 24 silk suits he had taken to Paris, and any other material that might be considered a vanity. Instead, he switched to austerity, as William Fitzstephen explains: 'Clad in a hair shirt of the roughest kind, which reached to his knees and swarmed with vermin, he mortified his flesh with the sparest diet, and his accustomed drink was water used for the cooking of hay…He would eat some of the meat placed before him, but fed chiefly on bread.'

Above: Thomas Becket took his role as Archbishop of Canterbury seriously: he washed the feet of beggars daily and wore a hair shirt.

In addition, Becket would wash the feet of 13 beggars in his private room every day and whip himself until his back was bloody. He would receive and clothe the needy and visit the cells of sick monks. The new Becket quickly became Henry's worst nightmare. The friend and ally installed as the king's champion at the religious court had done the unthinkable: he had found God.

Now Becket defied any royal edict that might take power away from the Church. A mere hint of a threat to the Church produced a tirade of pious vitriol from the Archbishop. Becket refused to expose the clergy to Henry's new royal courts. But the king was determined to bring the priests to heel. He was incensed when he learned that more than 100 members of the clergy had committed murder since he took the throne, but none had been punished.

Henry drew up the Constitutions of Clarendon, a 16-clause document that drew a clear line between Church and Crown and made it clear that the king's law would apply to *all* of his subjects. Henry then demanded that all Church leaders swear to abide by the constitutions, but Becket refused. This was war.

Henry stripped Becket of all the castles he had gifted to him as chancellor, and appealed to Pope Alexander to control his man. The pope agreed that Becket should uphold all of the 'laws and customs of the realm', and Henry demanded an audience with his archbishop to discuss this papal order. After several hours of Henry's threats, tantrums and browbeating, Becket conceded. But this was a trap. The next day Becket was handed a copy of the Constitutions of Clarendon that he had inadvertently agreed to.

Henry was not done with Becket. He accused him of embezzlement during his time as chancellor and began proceedings. Becket was one of the first clergymen to appear in Henry's royal court. He made his entrance by riding into the council chambers carrying a large cross. Several of his bishops tried to take the cross from him, telling

him that if Henry similarly brandished his sword then there could never be reconciliation. Becket did not stay to hear the verdict, but instead fled the courtroom and England, making a stormy crossing of the Channel to seek refuge with Louis VII. In France, Becket continued his life of ostentatious austerity and self-punishment; he would stand for hours in a freezing stream and went without medical treatment for a painful abscess in his throat.

After several botched reconciliations between Becket and Henry, Henry resorted to calculated insult. When his son Henry the Younger was made heir apparent in 1170, it was not the Archbishop of Canterbury who crowned him, but the Archbishop of York. In retaliation, Becket excommunicated the Archbishop of York and all the other priests present at the coronation. This, for Henry, was the final straw.

Above: Thomas Becket here refuses to sign the Constitutions of Clarendon, which Henry II had tricked him into agreeing to.

FAMILY BETRAYALS

Before the events of 29 December 1170, the murder of Becket
had probably crossed Henry's mind more than once. However,
nothing definitively links him with the crime. Regardless of his
intentions, Becket's death set in motion a series of catastrophic
events that would destroy Henry's family and threaten the entire
Plantagenet dynasty.

Henry had several heirs hovering at that time: Richard, John,
Geoffrey and of course Henry the Younger, who was Count of
Anjou and Maine, Duke of Normandy and King of England, in
name anyway. Henry II bestowed land and titles on two of his
other sons. Richard would receive the Dukedom of Aquitaine;
Geoffrey, the Dukedom of Brittany. John, the youngest, did not
receive anything. It is fair to use the phrase 'chip off the old
block' when considering Henry's sons: for all were energetic,
ambitious, quarrelsome and given to fits of rage when they did
not get their way.

Henry the Younger felt he had the worst of
it, after his father fled from the condemnation
over Becket and left him, the King of England,
to bear the brunt of the Plantagenet shame.
He had also largely been denied the trappings
expected of the king's office; he did not own
lands or have an income. He was also vain,
greedy and had gone deeply into debt to pay
for his lavish lifestyle.

To make matters worse, Henry II had gifted
his six-year-old son John, his favourite, the
castles Loudon, Mirebeau and Chinon, the
crowning glory of Anjou, of which Henry the
Younger was count. He retaliated by riding to
Paris and hatching a treasonous plot against his
father with King Louis VII.

Louis's hatred of Henry II was deep. Henry
had more money, land and power than Louis, even though he
was one of the king's subjects. He had also all but stolen Louis's
bride Eleanor and then done with her what Louis couldn't –

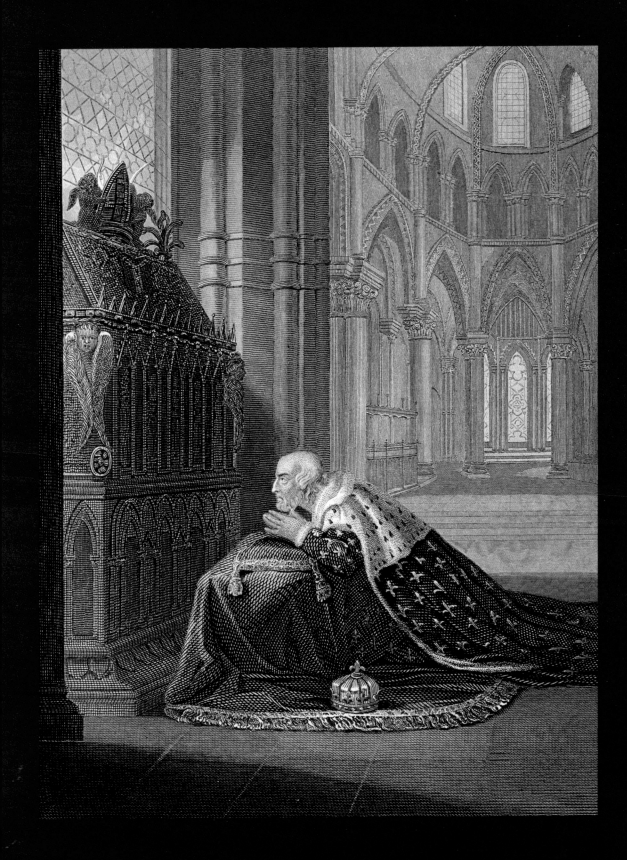

ELEANOR SPURNED

ELEANOR WAS ONE OF the most powerful and influential figures in 12th-century Europe; once her part in the rebellion was uncovered Henry could not risk granting her freedom. Gerald of Wales wrote that Henry 'imprisoned Queen Eleanor his wife as punishment for the destruction of their marriage... Then, again Count Geoffrey of Anjou when he was seneschal of France took advantage of Queen Eleanor; for which reason he often warned his son Henry, telling him above all not to touch her, they say this was because she was his lord's [Louis VII] wife, and because he had known her himself.'

Left: Eleanor of Aquitaine bucked the trend for women in the Middle Ages by being one of the most powerful and influential figures in Europe.

Gerald's words are typical of Christian medieval attitudes towards women: they were to be subservient and submissive to their husbands and, above all else, virgins. Sexually experienced women of the king's court, for example, could not bring an accusation of rape, and fornication outside a marriage was blamed entirely on the female. Women were, after all, the source of human lechery, according to the Church.

Henry tried to paint Eleanor as a harlot and temptress. However, the truth was that Eleanor was a formidable enemy and a threat to the prevailing belief that women gave up their freedom and rights to their husbands at marriage.

Paradoxically, notions of chivalrous love as told through the tales of Arthurian myth were fostered at the court of Eleanor. The queen was highly educated and cultivated and had a great influence on the development of 12th-century art and literature. Henry kept Eleanor a prisoner at court in England for 16 years, until his death. During that time and afterwards, her influence could still be felt across the Plantagenet kingdom.

produce several male heirs. Henry seemed to enjoy rubbing Louis's face in all of this; Becket's ostentatious visits to Paris were inspired by royal malice. Nothing would give the King of France more satisfaction than toppling Henry II.

Henry the Younger was not alone in his rebellion – his brothers Geoffrey and Richard also joined him in Paris. And behind the young princes was their mother Eleanor. Plotting with her sons against Henry II was certainly treason; forming an alliance with Louis VII of France was an act of war and an effective end to her marriage. Henry knew about the plot because his men had recognized and captured Eleanor as she rode disguised as a man from Aquitaine to Louis in Paris.

There was battle and bloodshed, both in France and in Britain, as Henry's enemies crawled out from the shadows to

Below: Henry II is shown fighting King William of Scotland at the 1174 Battle of Alnwick. The short battle ended in a defeat for the Scots.

join the rebellion against him. With their mother captured, Henry tried to reason with her sons. He rode up to the walls of Henry the Younger's stronghold to parley, but he only received a volley of arrows in return.

The worst bloodshed occurred in Britain, where a grand coalition of English barons joined with King William of Scotland and brought in the dreaded Flemish mercenaries to help with the butchery. Henry hired his own Brabanter mercenaries in 1174 and sailed to England with his army and the imprisoned Eleanor in tow.

HENRY HAD BEEN AT PAINS FOLLOWING THE MURDER OF BECKET TO CLAIM HIS DIVINE RIGHT TO RULE.

Their crossing was horrendous. With violent winds and huge waves crashing over Henry's ship, even the veteran sailors wondered aloud if they would make it alive. Henry stood before all on board and shouted that if God wanted him to live and restore his English kingdom, then they would make the crossing without harm. Their landing in Southampton seemed to prove him correct.

Henry had been at pains following the murder of Becket to claim his divine right to rule. However, the dead hand of Becket seemed behind all of his failed endeavours. He decided to put the Becket matter permanently to rest with the greatest publicity stunt of his reign. With this in mind, he rode to Canterbury Cathedral.

Opposite: Henry II prepares to receive his flogging from the monks of Canterbury Cathedral; many gathered to perform this task.

'*When he [Henry] reached Canterbury he leaped off his horse and, putting aside his royal dignity, he assumed the appearance of a pilgrim, a penitent, a supplicant, and on Friday 12 July, went to the cathedral. There, with streaming tears, groans and sighs, he made his way to the glorious martyr's tomb. Prostrating himself with his arms outstretched, he remained there a long time in prayer. He asked for absolution from the bishops then present, and subjected his flesh to harsh discipline from cuts with rods, receiving three or even five strokes from each of the monks in turn, of whom a large number had gathered.*'

– *PICTURES OF HISTORY*, RALPH DE DICETO

Henry's penance was a clever turn. The people of Canterbury were astounded to see their king in a hair shirt and barefoot

walking towards the cathedral. Henry's feet had been badly cut on the ragged, filthy medieval street; the monks, remembering Becket, gashed his back open with their whips.

The next morning, Henry, forced to lie still on his stomach as servants tended his wounds, heard the news that the Scottish king, William the Lion, had been captured and his army disbanded. Somehow, with Becket's ghost laid to rest, Henry's luck seemed to turn. He quickly overthrew the remaining rebels.

His son, Henry the Younger, died not as a hero fighting against his father's armies but of dysentery. Henry's famous remark about his son's passing was: 'He cost me much, but I wish he had lived to cost me more.'

After his penance at Canterbury, Henry was taken back into the papal fold, but only at the cost of conceding that the clergy would be tried only in Church courts. This practice became known as 'Benefit of Clergy' and those tried under it were never sentenced to death. Instead, if the accused could recite a short biblical text, usually the 51st Psalm, then they were immediately absolved of their crime. Henry's efforts for a fair justice system for all his English subjects had failed.

Below: The new king of France, Philip II, is shown here at the battle of Le Mans against Henry II. Philip's support of Henry's son Richard would lead to Henry's undoing.

Meanwhile, the newly reformed Henry forgave his family for their treachery – all, that is, except Eleanor. Geoffrey was killed during a jousting tournament in Paris. But remaining were Richard and John, known to history respectively as 'Lionheart' and 'The Evil King'.

As the eldest, it seemed fair that Richard could expect to be Henry's heir apparent. But Henry, who loved John more, refused to make the necessary arrangements. Perhaps predictably, Richard joined forces with the new French king, Philip II, and declared war against his father in France.

Henry's luck would not hold. Richard and Philip were young, ambitious and had the support of large armies. Henry, by comparison, was 50 – old by medieval standards – and he had little stomach left for further civil war. His legs famously bowed after a lifetime in the saddle, Henry had to be strapped on to his horse to parley with Richard and Philip and come to terms. In 1189, Henry agreed to give up all that he owned to his traitorous son; he had little choice. However, the old king's spark had not been entirely extinguished. He famously leaned into Richard's ear and growled: 'God grant that I may not die until I have my revenge on you.'

Henry was then carried on a litter to his court at Chinon Castle. Here, from his bed he was given a list of those who had pledged allegiance to Richard. At the top was the name of his other son and favourite, John. According to legend, Henry turned to face the wall heartbroken. He died soon afterwards in a fever, his final words were: 'shame, shame on a conquered king.'

Below: The tombs of King Henry II and the wife who betrayed him, Queen Eleanor of Aquitaine.

2

RICHARD I & JOHN

Richard the Lionheart was said to be truly happy only when his sword was covered with enemy blood. As a monarch, Richard differed little from his brother, the evil and hapless King John. Both men were violent and rapacious and determined to suck their dominions dry.

RICHARD I is often considered a true English hero: the chivalrous crusading king who battled the heathen Saladin for the Holy Land and brought honour and prestige to the English realm. In reality, Richard did not speak a word of English, spent only six months of his 10-year kingship in the country, and did his utmost during his reign to empty the national coffers. Richard's opinion of England was that it was 'cold and always raining' and there was nothing in the kingdom he wouldn't tax or sell to finance his warfare; he once remarked he would sell London if he could find a buyer.

Bloodshed was Richard's chief concern in life and fighting his main preoccupation since childhood. He had inherited the fiery Plantagenet hair and with it the height, strength and long arms seemingly purpose-built to wield a broadsword. He also had the

Opposite: A statue of Richard the Lionheart outside Westminster Palace, London. Often remembered as a great national hero, Richard actually cared little for England.

ferocious family temper and a reputation for extreme cruelty. His misdeeds included throwing three prisoners from a cliff to their deaths and blinding 15 others; his crusades abounded in atrocities.

Richard was once described by a contemporary chronicler as 'a bad son, a bad husband, a selfish ruler, and a vicious man.' Despite this, Richard began his reign with a rare moment of sentimentality. After being crowned King of England in 1189, Richard I visited his father's tomb at Fontevraud Abbey, where he fell upon Henry's stone effigy and wept. Blood was said to have streamed from the late king's nose – the mark of a murderer, according to medieval superstition.

Cynics would say Richard's outpouring was something of a publicity stunt. After all, the new king had committed treason against his late father and hurried his demise. To absolve himself of these crimes against king, country and family, Richard

Below: Richard I's coronation took place in Westminster Abbey on 3 September, 1189. It was the first full and detailed description of a coronation from this period.

requested a papal pardon from the Archbishop of Canterbury. In return, Richard suggested he could wage a crusade on the pope's behalf against Saladin, the Muslim king who had captured the holy city of Jerusalem in 1187. This was an agreeable arrangement for all parties, especially Richard, who would be kept away from the dreariness of English rule and back in his fighting saddle.

Richard was uninterested in England, to be sure, but it would be wrong to assume the king was disliked for this reason. In the violence and instability of the Middle Ages, people liked a powerful military-minded king. Success in battle brought prestige and glory; it also implied that God was smiling favourably on the victor. Being victorious in war fitted neatly with the emerging ideals of chivalry, a warrior code centred on honour, courtly love and valour in battle.

Chivalry had its heart in the medieval reimagining of King Arthur and his Round Table of gallant knights. Richard's mother Eleanor loved this entirely English story and fed her sons on the new Arthurian tales of chivalry and war.

> IN PRACTICE, THE IDEALS OF MEDIEVAL CHIVALRY WERE VAGUE AND FLUID: LAW, JUSTICE AND REASON WERE OFTEN OVERRULED IN ITS NAME.

In practice, the ideals of medieval chivalry were vague and fluid: law, justice and reason were often overruled in its name. In the Holy Land, for example, the lives of enemy knights and nobles could be spared for reasons of chivalry while whole communities of unarmed women and children were indiscriminately slaughtered. Chivalry and the will of a Christian God were great enablers of crusading violence.

Almost as soon as the English crown was on Richard I's head he began organizing his crusade against Saladin. This would cost vast sums; Richard spent three months in England – half the duration of his time there – selling, taxing, borrowing and seizing. Nothing was sacred; Richard was described by contemporary chroniclers as 'behaving like a robber, always looking for something to steal'; 'he put up for sale all that he had, offices, lordships, earldoms, sheriffdoms, castles, towns, lands, everything.' No one was exempt from the taxes, not even the Church for whom the campaign was mounted.

THE PLANTAGENET ARTHUR

ACCORDING TO LEGEND, King Arthur was a British king who fought against the Anglo-Saxons after the fall of Rome. There is no evidence that he really existed. However, the 6th-century Welsh monk Gildas wrote about a Romano-British leader named Ambrosius Aurelianus who 'wore purple' and defeated the Anglo-Saxons at the Battle of Badon. It is thought the name Aurelianus may have become Arthur by the time of his first mention in the 9th-century *Historia Brittonum* (History of the Britons).

The *Historia Brittonum* was the first British text to suggest Britain had been settled by Brutus, a descendant of Aeneas the Trojan who, according to the poet Virgil, had escaped the fall of Troy and later founded Rome. The text was used as the basis for Geoffrey of Monmouth's *Historia regum Britanniae* and subsequently the *Roman de Brut*, a Plantagenet text by Wace, commissioned by Henry II for his wife, Eleanor of Aquitaine. This French interest in English stories can perhaps be explained by the Plantagenet part in the history of the country: they were, after all, now the rulers of England.

In the world of Arthur in the *Roman de Brut* and romances written by Chrétien de Troyes, the knights of the Round Table are sent on mysterious quests that involve brushes with the supernatural and the liberation of distressed damsels. This literature of knightly valour and loyalty was the cultural inheritance of Richard and his brother John: treason, betrayal of the family bond and murder were three of the ways in which the brothers interpreted the ideals of chivalry in real life.

Right: This engraving shows 12th-century French poet Chrétien de Troyes in his studio.

The collection of crusading funds was combined with a wave of bigotry targeted at English Jews and their property. Many joined in this persecution with glee: a mob went on a rampage in London, ransacking Jewish houses and murdering their occupants. The slaughter reached a climax in York, when 150 Jews sheltering in a castle tower committed suicide rather than face massacre by an attacking mob; those who did not die by their own hand were burned alive. Richard denounced the atrocities, but his pursuit of the guilty was tepid.

While crusading fever ended in the murder of some subjects, none were exempt from the taxations imposed upon them. England would not quickly forget being fleeced by Richard the Lionheart. Rising levels of tax were matched by a steep increase in prices. The high cost of living harmed ordinary people and inflamed even barons who could afford to meet it. Magna Carta would be their revenge.

Richard did not live to see Magna Carta, and nor would the thought of such an uprising have occurred to him; he went on stripping England of wealth and men. To raise a fleet of 100 English ships Richard spent over £14,000, or more than half of his annual revenue from England. Royal accounts provide lists of supplies put on board: cheeses, beans, arrows, crossbow bolts, 60,000 horseshoes and 14,000 cured pig carcasses. It is estimated that Richard's force raised from his vast lands in England and France totalled 219 ships and 17,000 soldiers and sailors.

As Duke of Aquitaine, Richard's territories in France covered a quarter of the country. Combined with England, this 'Angevin Empire', as it is sometimes known, was a high point of the

Above: An illustration of a rampaging mob in London during a particularly brutal period of anti-Semitism under Richard I.

Plantagenets' dominion. It also put Richard, in terms of wealth and power, above that of the King of France, Philip II. It was with Philip that Richard had arranged to launch the crusade against Saladin, but they would be allies in name only. Richard alienated many other fellow crusaders with his pomposity and arrogance.

CRUSADING KINGS

En route to the Holy Land, Richard infuriated Philip by reneging on an agreement to marry his sister, Alice. Instead, on his mother's instruction, Richard married Berengaria of Navarre, whom Eleanor herself had delivered to Richard's temporary base in Sicily. Enraged, Philip sailed ahead to Jerusalem; he would not forgive the humiliation.

> RICHARD'S ATROCITY WOULD LIVE LONG IN THE COLLECTIVE MUSLIM MEMORY.

Philip and the other crusaders of Europe, however, would need Richard's help. When Richard joined the crusaders in 1191, allegedly wielding a sword called Excalibur, he found them unsuccessfully besieging the city of Acre. Encamped around the thick city walls held by Saladin were crusaders including Philip and Leopold V of Austria. Attacks on the walls using fire, arrows and siege machine missiles had weakened the city defences, but every time the walls were breached Saladin led a fierce counteroffensive that gave him time to rebuild.

The result was a terrible war of attrition. Rotting carcasses had been piled up in the castle moat to enable skirmishes on the walls; starving European soldiers ate their pack horses and mules; Muslim warriors slung flaming missiles at the attacking siege engines; the sky was dark with smoke and arrows.

Richard himself was suffering with Arnaldia, a form of scurvy that was causing his teeth and hair to fall out, but nothing could stop his siege of the city. In an attempt to break the deadlock, Richard and Philip invited Saladin to parley, and it was agreed that the Muslim king would release 1500 Christian captives as a sign of good faith. But when the allotted day came Saladin reneged on the deal. In response, Richard beheaded 2700 Muslim prisoners before the city walls. Saladin, in turn, murdered the prisoners he had promised to free.

Opposite: By marrying Berengaria of Navarre, Richard I broke an earlier marriage agreement to marry Philip II of France's sister and made Philip an enemy for life.

The memory of Richard's atrocity would live long in the collective Muslim memory. Mothers threatened naughty children by saying: 'Be good or the King of England will come to get you'; the crusaders were described as brave fighters but little more than vicious animals in every other respect. In the end, Richard conquered Acre and defeated Saladin in a pitched battle near Jerusalem. This marked the end of Richard's crusade: the holy city itself was of little real interest to the English king, and his brother was causing trouble at home. So Richard departed for England.

The problem for Richard was that he had made more enemies than friends while abroad. For this reason he had to travel back to England overland disguised as a pilgrim, but spies working for Leopold of Austria ambushed and arrested him. Richard had

Below: Richard I and Philip II are depicted outside the walls of the freshly conquered Acre. After defeating Saladin in battle, Richard sailed home.

upset Leopold by occupying a Muslim palace already claimed by the Austrian. The final insult had been when Richard tore down Leopold's royal banners and replaced them with his own. Richard was imprisoned in a castle overlooking the Danube and then sold on to King Henry VI of Germany.

All of this was music to the ears of Philip II of France who, like Leopold, had been humiliated by Richard. Philip had cut his crusade short when it was clear that Richard was the better general; he hated the Plantagenet for it. Now Philip did a deal with Richard's brother John: John would swear his fealty to Philip II in return for help in securing the English throne. Naively, John threw in a swathe of Aquitaine land as a gesture of goodwill. This land would never be permanently recovered by the Plantagenets.

John had already exposed his ambition for the crown by constantly undermining the authority of the bishops left behind to run England in Richard's stead. Now he announced that Richard had been killed in captivity and that he would be taking over. No one believed John, and the bishops quickly raised an army against him. Before a blow was struck, however, news came from King Henry VI that he wanted 34 tons of silver in return for Richard's release: a king's ransom indeed.

Richard and John's mother Eleanor set about accumulating the ransom while Philip and John did all they could to keep him in captivity. Philip even offered Henry VI double the ransom to keep him locked up, but Henry instead accepted the original ransom paid by Eleanor. The money had been raised by a 25 per cent tax on all income in England and the removal of

Above: Richard I confronts King Henry VI of Germany. Richard had been sold to Henry by Leopold of Austria, one of the European monarchs he had upset in the Holy Land.

any ecclesiastical treasure that could be taken from the churches; England was once again paying through the nose for Richard. Now, their king was a free man.

In 1194, Philip sent John a message: 'Look to yourself. The devil is loosed.' According to legend, one of the barons supporting John literally died of fright when the dead king landed near his castle on the coast near Sandwich. Richard, however, did not punish John, who met his brother with open arms and a fulsome apology. It is perhaps telling that while the

Right: John begs Richard for forgiveness after conspiring against him with Philip II. Surprisingly, there were no familial reprisals.

Opposite: A woodcut of knights battling in a medieval tournament melee.

MEDIEVAL TOURNAMENTS

MEDIEVAL TOURNAMENTS WERE A great proving ground for young knights wishing to display their prowess. The tournaments consisted mainly of the melee – a dangerous free-for-all between two groups of knights: the visitors, or 'attackers', and the hosts, 'the defenders'.

The battlefield itself was an area between two towns that included the open countryside, villages, woods and anything else that happened to be in the way. The purpose of the melee was to capture knights from the opposing team, confiscate their equipment and horses and hold them to ransom. The ransomed knight would only be released upon promise of future payment. The team that captured the most was the winner, and capturers could earn themselves a small fortune in the process.

There were only two rules: knights were not supposed to injure or kill each other; and nobody could be attacked while taking shelter in one of the fenced-off recets, or rest areas. There were, however, no officials at the melees to enforce the rules, and so there were often serious injuries and fatalities. At one tournament, 60 combatants were killed in a particularly brutal summer melee, many of them suffocating in the dust of the battlefield. Rumours spread that demons in the form of crows and vultures had circled the field as the knights perished. The knights were not the only ones at risk – villagers and other bystanders caught up in the action would suffer injuries of their own, often under the hooves of a galloping horse.

Richard I himself was a great participant of the tournaments, but disliked the damage large melees did to the countryside. However, he overturned his father Henry II's earlier ban on the tournaments and legalized them under royal licence. Their worth as a recruiting ground for knights was too good an opportunity to be missed.

great warlord did not think of John as any real threat, he also recognized that the Plantagenet legacy was more important than a bit of royal backstabbing and family betrayal.

Richard would not, however, accept the loss of his French lands, and raised a new army to reclaim them. He picked the best knights in his English kingdom using the great recruitment tool of the medieval age: the tournament. After a few months, Richard sailed to France to war with Philip; he would not return to England.

RICHARD'S END

Richard was said to charge at the French forces now occupying his Plantagenet lands as 'a lion craving food runs at its prey'. He was immediately successful, taking several castles. Philip, in turn, reinvaded territories and both men pillaged as they went.

Right: Richard I here defeats Philip II in a miniature from William of Tyre's *Historia Ierosolimitana.*

The kings also adopted the practice of putting out the eyes of captives who displayed loyalty to the opposing side; serfs and peasants were among the victims of this savage punishment.

Richard and Philip famously came face to face several years later at Gisors. Archdeacon Ralph de Diceto describes the meeting:

'Richard King of the English entered the territory of the king of the French with a large army on 27 September and took the castles of Courcelles, Burriz and Sirefontaine. On the next day the King of France came from Mantes with four hundred knights and sergeants with their supplies to help the castle of Courcelles, which he did not think was captured. Therefore the king of the English, as soon as he saw him coming, pursued him as they turned back in flight, and placed him in such straits at the gates of Gisors that the bridge was broken under him, with twenty knights drowned.'

– *PICTURES OF HISTORY*, RALPH DE DICETO

Above: King Richard lies on his death bed after being struck in the shoulder by a crossbow bolt.

At Gisors, Philip was said to have 'drunk of the river' and struggled for his life. A truce between Philip and Richard was hastily agreed, but the Plantagenet would not rest. Instead he rode his army to Limousin to fight the rebellious Viscount of Limoges. Richard put the land to fire and sword and besieged the rather insignificant castle of Châlus-Chabrol. After three days the walls of the castle were close to collapse when a bolt from a crossbow caught Richard in the shoulder. The king snapped the bolt in two, but the point could not be extracted 'without great violence'. Twelve days later, Richard, the great hero of chivalry and warfare, died of septicaemia. His body was buried at Fontevraud, next to Henry, the father he had betrayed.

ENTER EVIL KING JOHN

Before he became King of England in 1199, John's nickname was 'Lackland', simply because, as youngest son to Henry II, there was no available family land left to bequeath to him. Despite this, John had always been Henry II's favourite, although he had

betrayed his father at the behest of Richard, the brother whose shadow he never shook off. Richard was tall, handsome and could not be bettered on the battlefield. John was stocky, around 30cm (12in) shorter than Richard, and had a great love of fine clothes, jewellery and taking baths, a rarity for that time. Richard was painted by contemporary chroniclers as a chivalrous, dashing man of action; John was described as indecisive, untrustworthy and having an unlikeable demeanour; he would often snigger with his entourage at the misery of others.

In modern times there has been a great historical levelling between Richard and John: after all, both men were equally capable of heinous cruelty and violence. However, John has never escaped popular infamy for his crimes.

Above: This portrait of King John reveals his likeness to father Henry II. In reality, the pair could not have been more different.

John had gone to great pains to undermine his brother's rule while Richard was on crusade. He had openly rebelled against Richard's appointed government, including his bishops and the justiciar William de Longchamp, who John forced into exile. John supported plans for a Scottish invasion of England and connived with King Philip II of France to keep Richard locked up abroad.

Philip, however, did not support John's accession after Richard's death, instead backing the claim of Arthur, John's nephew. Son to Henry II's son, Geoffrey, Arthur was something of a chip off the Plantagenet block. At 15 he was already attacking family members for private gain. He joined forces with Philip in besieging his grandmother Eleanor of Aquitaine in her castle of Mirebeau, in Poitiers.

John secured the English crown with all haste and then marched his army over 140 km (87 miles) towards Poitiers in just two days. He then surrounded the besieging army, liberated his

mother Eleanor and imprisoned Arthur in Normandy. Visiting
Arthur's dungeon cell, John found his nephew to be defiant
and unrepentant. Arthur demanded John hand over the English
crown or be subjected to a lifetime of misery at his hand.

Arthur's threats were a naive blunder: the Plantagenet teenager
would never be seen again. One rumour was that John had had
Arthur castrated but the surgery was so badly botched that he
died from blood loss. Another said four knights were dispatched
to end his life, just as four had ended Thomas Becket's. The most
reliable claim came from Arthur's jailor, in the employ of William
de Braose, the baron of the castle where Arthur was imprisoned.

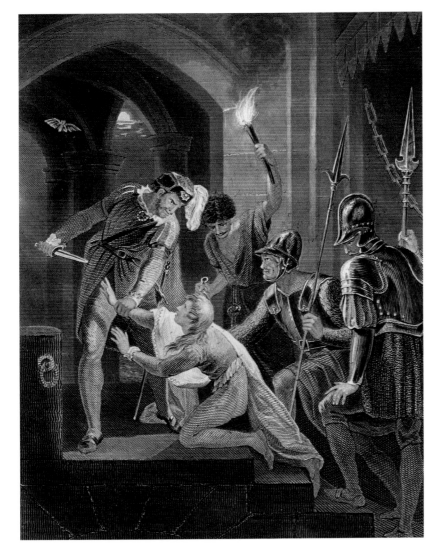

Left: Prince Arthur is
here killed by his uncle,
John. In reality, John
was more likely to have
undertaken the task alone.

The story went that after dinner one night, a drunken John went to Arthur's cell and ran him through. He attached a stone to his dead nephew's corpse and threw it in the River Seine. The news of Arthur's alleged murder did John a great disservice: many of his French barons renounced their allegiance and switched to Philip; Philip himself said he would not stop his campaign against John until Arthur was produced, something he probably knew to be an impossibility.

The end result would be absolute loss of all Plantagenet lands in France except for Gascony, an isolated patch on the southwest border. Eleanor herself died at 82 as the once mighty Angevin Empire crumbled and Philip's troops closed in on her at Fontevraud Abbey. She was buried there in 1204, alongside Henry, the husband she had betrayed and Richard, her favourite son. John spent the remaining years of his reign unsuccessfully trying to win back his French territories. He was lucky to hold on to his English kingdom as he did so.

England would pay for John's follies. His subjects groaned under the weight of the king's taxes. The winter of 1204/05 had been particularly harsh, the Thames famously freezing over as crops failed in the ice and snow; famine soon took hold. There were murmurs that God was punishing John and England for the king's failures in France. Many barons balked at the idea that they should pay to help John retrieve the land.

William Marshal, one of the few barons to remain faithful to John, warned him not to attempt an invasion of France. John tried nevertheless; by the summer of 1205 he had failed. He simply did not have enough support to restore the family empire.

John would not forgive his English barons' resistance to his dynastic ambitions: to keep England paying he went on long tours of the country, seizing properties and inventing new taxes as he went. John became like Henry II, constantly on the move: a train of packhorses and carts transported the king's retinue from one place to the next; he had a portable dining table and chapel that could be set up by any roadside.

Castle lords soon became ready for a visit from John at little notice; the finest of everything was naturally expected. This

OWNERSHIP OF WOMEN AND WIVES WAS WELL WITHIN THE KING'S REMIT.

WILLIAM MARSHAL

DESCRIBED AS 'the greatest knight who ever lived', William Marshal was an English baron and paragon of chivalry during the turbulent reigns of Henry II, Richard I, John and Henry III. He was one of the few to remain faithful to John after the loss of his French lands and was a vital cog in the machinery of Magna Carta.

Born in 1146, William was sent out as a child hostage by his father John Marshal as Stephen besieged the castle during the Anarchy. Stephen shouted out that he would hang William in front of the castle walls if Marshal didn't give himself up. Marshal told him to go ahead, saying: 'I have a hammer and anvil to make more and better sons.' William was spared and grew into a formidable fighter with an uncanny ability for the tournament – he made himself rich and famous and become a friend of Henry the Younger as the two toured the tournament circuits of Europe.

Marshal served with Henry II against his son Richard and even had the chance of killing Richard after ambushing and unhorsing him, the only man ever to do so. But he refrained from killing Richard and instead slayed his horse, just to make his point. Richard did not forget this mercy and upon becoming King Richard I honoured Marshal by arranging his marriage to Isabel de Clare, Countess of Pembroke. This made Marshal the Earl of Pembroke and one of the wealthiest men in the country. Marshal was also named Lord Protector, and went on to serve John when he became king. Despite hostilities between Marshal and John, Marshal served loyally and helped his heir, Henry III, take the throne after his death.

Above: This effigy of William Marshal comes from his tomb in the Temple Church, London.

included the king's sexual access to wives and daughters. Those who denied John his advances were often summarily punished. The wife of Hugh de Neville was ordered to pay the Crown 200 chickens so she could rejoin her husband in the marital bed for just one night. Ownership of women and wives was well within the king's remit.

Other taxes rained upon the English barons, including Crown fees for the granting of inheritances or royal permission for noblewomen to marry. Many barons had to pay a scutage tax to prevent their offspring being sent away on military service; William de Braose had to pay 300 cows and 10 horses for the privilege.

William de Braose had once been a favourite of John's, but had fallen badly out of favour. This may have been because William's wife, Maud, made no secret of the fact that she knew John had murdered his nephew, Arthur (the Plantagenet prince had died while imprisoned in William de Braose's castle and the jailor had told all). William had once been tipped to become the most powerful baron in England, but now John set out to destroy him with ruinous taxes.

Below: John's army is here undone by Philip at the 1214 Battle of Bouvines.

When the money was not forthcoming, John began seizing William's castles and jailed his eldest son as collateral against the debt. Maud knew what happened to young nobles in John's captivity and the family prepared to flee to Ireland. However, Maud and her son, also called William, were caught en route and duly imprisoned. After a few weeks, John cut off their supply of food. After 11 days the pair were found to have starved to death; William's cheeks had been eaten away by his ravenous mother.

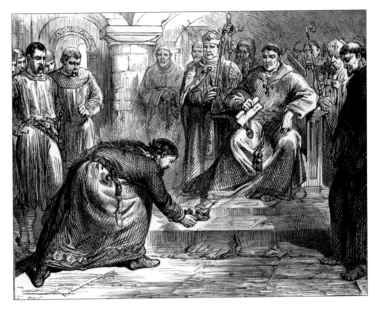

Above: John bows before the pope's legate in 1213 in his quest for papal forgiveness.

The news confirmed the extent of John's cruelty and was perhaps the greatest mistake he made during his reign. His crime led directly to one of the defining clauses of Magna Carta: 'No man shall be taken, imprisoned, outlawed, banished or in any way destroyed, nor will we proceed against or prosecute him, except by the lawful judgement of his peers or by the law of the land.'

John's crusade in France ended with rout at the hands of Philip at the Battle of Bouvines in 1214; he returned to England in disgrace. But it was not the military humiliation that hurt John's barons most, it was the colossal cost.

A group of 39 of 197 barons now rode out against John. With them was Stephen Langton, the Archbishop of Canterbury, expelled from the country by John in 1207. He persuaded Pope Innocent III to put the country under an interdict forbidding all church services, including burials and baptisms. For six years, no church bells were heard in England. In an age of belief, the loss of church services undermined popular support for the king. Many of his subjects began to despise him.

John responded to the pope's decree by jailing the priests' mistresses and stealing all the ecclesiastical treasure he could find.

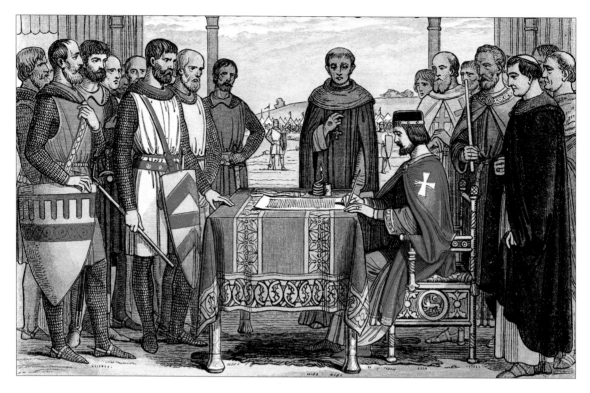

Above: John signs
Magna Carta in 1215 at
Runnymede, a meadow
near Windsor.

He would never return this fortune to the Church. However, he
had to beg for the pope's forgiveness in 1213 after Innocent III
called for John to be deposed and asked Philip II of France to
carry out the order.

John had been officially pardoned by Stephen Langton,
whom the king had allowed back to England as part of his
reconciliation with Rome. Now Langton was insisting John
should sign Magna Carta, the Great Charter, so called for its
length rather than its importance. The terms of the 63-clause
document were to confirm the barons' feudal rights, declare
the monarch to be subject to the rule of law and document the
liberties held by all 'free men'. In simple terms, the charter would
prevent the barons from being molested in their own lands and
exempt them from arbitrary royal taxes.

Magna Carta is often considered a groundbreaking symbol of
England's constitutional liberty, but it was a great failure at the
time. John tried to fob the barons off, saying he would consider
Magna Carta later; after a long period of delay he agreed to sign.
This famously took place in 1215 at Runnymede, a meadow

THE HOODED MAN

MAGNA CARTA STATED THAT the king's forests would be opened and Forest Law alleviated. Before then, the forests of England were the exclusive domain of the English monarch, as were the animals and greenery on which they fed. Hunting the king's deer was a crime punishable by having two fingers removed for a first offence and having eyes put out for a second. The outlaw who famously flouted these rules by dining on the king's deer, living in the royal Sherwood forests and robbing from the rich to give to the poor was, of course, the legendary Robin Hood.

Robin Hood supposedly existed during the 12th century, while Richard was away on crusade and John was pillaging the land. However, there is no direct historical evidence of Robin Hood, nor is there consensus on where he lived – scholars variously place him in Barnsdale in southern Yorkshire, as well as the traditional Sherwood Forest in Nottingham. The first direct reference to the legend of Robin Hood does not appear until 1377, when the Scottish chronicler John of Fordun refers to a Robin Hood fighting for Simon de Montfort, a rebel baron from the time of Henry III. There is also a record of a fugitive called Robin Hood failing to appear before a royal justice in 1225, although 'Robin' and 'hood' – or a maker of hoods – were both common names in medieval England.

Above: Robin Hood and his men entertain Richard I in Sherwood Forest.

Above: A copy of Magna Carta, which is kept in the British Library in London.

near Windsor, where the king and barons exchanged kisses and signatures. William Marshal was one of the few barons still loyal to John to sign the document.

Although he signed the parchment at Runnymede, John had no intention of honouring any part of Magna Carta. He was simply playing for time while he worked out how to crush the barons. He appealed to Pope Innocent III to excommunicate the rebellious barons, which the pope duly did. However, Stephen Langton refused to publish the edict, which in turn led to his own suspension from duties.

The Barons' War between the barons and the king broke out in 1215. At first John gained the upper hand, seizing the Cornish lands of the leading rebel Robert Fitzwalter and occupying his castles. When several of the rebels holed up in Rochester Castle, John herded pigs with torches strapped to their backs into tunnels bolstered with wood below the castle.

For a time it appeared that John, who had been consistently derided for his military incompetence abroad, was going to win this war at home. However, rebel barons seized London and called on Philip II of France for help, promising the English crown to Philip's son Louis, on the grounds that the prince's wife had Plantagenet blood.

Louis landed at Dover, marched his army to Winchester and captured the castle there almost unopposed. Many who had previously been loyal to John now turned their coats to Louis; divine providence seemed to be on the side of the French prince.

Meanwhile, John tried desperately to avoid his enemies by leading a vast cavalcade through the East Anglian estuary known as the Wash. Here the carts famously sank into the marshy ground as the tide came in. The English monk Ralph of Coggeshall describes the event:

'He lost on these travels at the Wellstream his portable chapel with his relics and some of his pack-horses with many household supplies. And many members of his entourage were submerged in the waters of the sea and sucked into the quicksand because they had set out foolishly and in haste before the tide had receded.'

– *CHRONICON ANGLICANUM*, RALPH OF COGGESHALL

All of John's treasure was lost as the sea closed in; even, it was said, his crown jewels. It was the end for John. The king died of a fever and dysentery at Newark Castle and was later buried at Worcester Cathedral. He was 49 and among the most hated monarchs in living memory, or so his chroniclers wrote at the time. 'Hell herself,' said the Benedictine monk Matthew Paris, 'felt defiled by his admission'.

Left: King John's tomb at Worcester Cathedral. He remains a generally disliked monarch to this day.

•HENRY•III•

3

HENRY III

Henry III was not a ruthless warrior king like his father or grandfather. Instead, he was a pious, ponderous sovereign whose impressionability constantly undermined his rule. He was forever at odds with the strong characters he installed at court.

Henry III was nine when he was crowned in 1216 following the death of his father, John. The coronation took place at Gloucester Abbey rather than Westminster because London was still occupied by the French prince Louis, who had taken control during the Barons' War with the king. John had famously lost his crown jewels, so Henry had to be crowned with a headband of gold borrowed from his mother.

On his deathbed, John had made the Earl of Pembroke William Marshal swear to look after Henry. Nothing was certain at this time and the fate of the Plantagenet dynasty rested with Henry's protectors. Once described as the 'greatest knight who ever lived,' Marshal had consistently proven his loyalty to the crown. He promised John he would be the guardian of the young king: 'By God's sword, if all abandoned the king, do you know

Opposite: Henry III is shown with the golden-red Plantagenet hair in a stained-glass window from Bridgnorth Town Hall, Shropshire.

what I would do? I would carry him on my shoulders step by step, from island to island, from country to country, and I would not fail him not even if it meant begging my bread.'

This was typically chivalrous talk from Marshal, but he was true to his word. Marshal was the solid patriarchal figure that Henry would look for in all of his future companions at court. Henry reigned for 56 years, more than any other medieval king, and yet he needed others to do his fighting for him. He was submissive, impulsive and highly suggestible; his opinions were usually those of the last person he had spoken to.

Henry was an aesthete and a daydreamer who liked the idea of expanding his domain but constantly failed through poor judgment and incompetence. Many believed him to be a simpleton; his drooping eyelid and increasingly rotund figure played into this image. He was also petulant and given to the usual Plantagenet tantrums: he once tore the clothes off one of his court jesters and threw another into the River Thames. Henry was highly religious and attended mass whenever possible; he was said to be unable to pass a church holding a service without stopping to attend. His journeys often took several hours longer than necessary as a result.

Above: The young Henry III is presented to the English barons by William Marshal, his protector.

Henry's reliance on others perhaps arose from the guiding hand of his council of regents appointed by John. The council was full of strong leaders and included Peter des Roches, the Bishop of Winchester; the justiciar, Hubert de Burgh; and William Marshal.

The first act of the regents was to rid the country of Louis and defeat the English barons who still supported him. Marshal took the lead, attacking Louis at Lincoln Castle in 1217 and capturing many of his English allies. Some of Marshal's men then gleefully ransacked the town in the so-called 'Lincoln Fair', despite the town having always been faithful to the crown.

The Battle of Lincoln was the turning point in the Barons' War and almost the end of Louis, who fled to London and sued for terms of surrender. There was, however, a twist, as Louis's wife Blanche of Castile had assembled an armada of 80 ships in Calais with 100 knights and their men. News came to Louis that the armada had set sail for England on 24 August 1217. A hastily assembled fleet of 40 ships commanded by Hubert de Burgh set out to head them off. De Burgh's opposite number was an ex-Benedictine monk turned pirate: Eustace, the scourge of English merchant ships in the Channel.

Eustace was a type of anti-Robin Hood driven into outlawry; he had apparently studied necromancy in Toledo. He often blinded and mutilated his enemies, sometimes put his horse's shoes on backwards to confuse his pursuers, and once accepted a groat to perform sexual favours while dressed as a woman. Eustace was used to long, dirty street fights and, like many on the eve of war, believed himself destined to defeat the English at the Battle of Sandwich.

Above: Blanche of Castile assembled an armada to rescue her husband, King Louis, from England.

The Battle of Sandwich was the end for Louis. He accepted £7000 from William Marshal in exchange for quitting London and agreed to give Henry's Plantagenet lands back to him when he became King of France. Louis would not make good on this promise. Expelling the Frenchman would be Marshal's last service to the Plantagenet crown, and he died in 1219.

A year later, Henry had a full coronation at Westminster Abbey and confirmed Magna Carta in front of his barons. When he turned 16 in 1223, Henry assumed full control of the

THE BATTLE OF SANDWICH

HUBERT DE BURGH TOOK command of the small English fleet on the morning of 24 August as William Marshal stayed on shore to ready a landing party in the case of an English defeat. De Burgh's strategy was to head for the superior French fleet at full sail, as if he intended to engage them. He then ordered his ships to sail directly past the French through the gaps in their line. Eustace ordered his ships to sail into the Thames estuary and come to Louis's aid in London. However, the temptation to sink the apparently inferior English fleet was also strong.

As his enemies talked, De Burgh revealed the second part of his plan, which was to turn his ships and sail upon the French, who were now downwind. Rows of archers now revealed themselves on deck and sent out waves of volleys at the French ships. Pots of quicklime were hurled on to the French decks, blinding and bewildering the enemy. The English ships then pulled up alongside while soldiers leapt aboard to butcher their foes. The battle ended with the complete rout of Eustace and his fleet; the leader himself was decapitated and his body paraded through the streets of Dover and Sandwich.

Above: The Battle of Sandwich was a famous naval victory for the English over the French.

Left: The severed head
of ex-Benedictine monk,
pirate and necromancer,
Eustace, is paraded
through Dover.

crown and was no longer reliant on his regents. He immediately
made plans to expand his borders and put up great buildings;
he floated various other schemes that were suggested to him. A
contemporary once said of Henry: 'His mind seemed not to stand
on a firm basis, for every sudden accident put him into passion.'

Henry enjoyed the trappings of royalty and tried to impress
the court with ostentatious displays of his kingship. These
included elaborate religious rituals, long banquets and displays
of beautiful things, including sumptuous clothes and jewellery,
exotic animals from abroad and holy relics.

pres son regna henry le tert sun fiz. lvi. aunz. si
fuit de. ix. aunz de age quant fuit corone. E en fun
tens fuit la bataylle de Euelim. ou fuit occys syr
Symund de munfort. e sun fiz henry. e syre hugh le de
penser e muz des barons e des cheualers de Engle
tere. puis mourit cyl henry le roy. e gist a Westmuster.

Henry was a daydreamer who lived beyond his means. He was poor compared with John or Henry II. The vast revenue that used to come from the Angevin Empire had dwindled after the loss of the Plantagenet lands in France. Henry was also frustrated by Magna Carta: he couldn't simply impose taxes when he wanted cash, as Richard and John had done. The barons controlled how much coin flowed into the royal coffers; if they disagreed with how it was being spent they simply cut off the money supply.

The simple matter of cost seemed beyond Henry's comprehension. Early in his reign, he decided he should win back his family's territories in Normandy. His barons, however, did not share his dynastic ambitions and most refused to provide money or men. So Henry went it alone, hoping the local population would rise up in his favour. It did not. He marched his army around the region but did not succeed in actually engaging the enemy. Those watching said Henry's army looked as though it was performing a military procession or drill. After a few uneventful weeks, Henry sailed home again. His uncle, Richard the Lionheart, must have turned in his grave.

Henry's problem was that he no longer had a strongman such as William Marshal to provide military advice or lead his armies. He did have someone in mind as a replacement, though. This was a French knight named Simon de Montfort who had arrived at the English court wishing to stake a claim for the earldom of Leicester, which he viewed as his birthright.

De Montfort was a religious fanatic who wore a hair shirt, abstained from worldly pleasures and was known to stay up all night in prayer. He had spent time slaying heretics in Toulouse with his father and was considered a clever battlefield tactician. He was also driven and ambitious. Henry liked him immediately.

In a friendship that echoed that of Henry II and Thomas Becket, de Montfort became Henry's instant favourite. Henry allowed de Montfort to rise quickly up the social ladder: he made

Left: A 13th-century illustration of the coronation of King Henry III.

Above: This medieval illustration shows the 1236 marriage of Henry III to Eleanor of Provence.

him Earl of Leicester and give his sister Eleanor in marriage. This created a great scandal: Eleanor was the catch of Europe and should have been saved for a marriage with an important king on the continent. She had also taken a vow of chastity after the death of her previous husband, William Marshal the Younger. Many barons, including Henry and Eleanor's brother Richard, Earl of Cornwall, opposed the union. In the end, Richard had to be placated with a cash gift from Henry.

Henry had kept Eleanor's dowry for himself rather than giving it to his new best friend, Simon de Montfort. This was a problem for de Montfort, whose rapid rise through the ranks

Right: Here, Simon de Montfort argues with Henry III. The former best friends had a famous falling out.

of the nobility had cost him a fortune. He soon realized his
new wife was used to living in luxury. De Montfort had had to
borrow heavily from Henry of Savoy, the brother of Henry's
wife, Eleanor of Provence, to cover his debts. Perhaps naively, he
had used Henry's name as a guarantor against this loan, but had
not informed the king.

When Henry found out he exploded with rage. At first, de
Montfort tried to shrug it off, but Henry would not be placated.
'You seduced my sister, and when I discovered this, I gave her
to you, against my will, to avoid scandal,' Henry ranted at his
friend. More accusations followed; the de Montforts had no
choice but to flee England for France. Those with long memories
at the English court knew the consequences of stoking
the Plantagenet anger.

But Henry and de Montfort were somehow
inextricably linked: their power struggles set a pattern
for the English monarchy for many centuries. Both
men would openly rue the day they met the other.

THEIR POWER STRUGGLES SET A PATTERN FOR THE ENGLISH MONARCHY FOR MANY CENTURIES.

FOREIGN FORAYS

Failing to remember the lesson of his Normandy invasion
12 years earlier, Henry now set out to reclaim the former
Plantagenet territory of Poitou. The barons of this region had
recently rebelled against the new king of France, Louis IX,
grandson of Philip II. One of the barons was Hugh de Lusignan,
Henry's stepfather. The Lusignans asked for Henry's help, with
the spoils to be divided equally.

Henry put his case for war to the English barons, and once
again they rejected it. Just as with his excursion to Normandy,
Henry would have to pay for the Poitou campaign from his own
pocket. In 1242, the king set sail for France accompanied by
200 knights. It would be a calamitous affair.

At Poitou, Henry was betrayed by his supposed allies and
utterly outdone by Louis IX on the battlefield: Henry was in fact
the worst general the Plantagenets had yet produced. He had
to plead with none other than Simon de Montfort to come and
bail him out. De Montfort acquiesced and even fought a brave

Above: The 1242 Battle of Taillebourg was a famous victory for the French over Henry III that ended his plans for Poitou.

rearguard action against Louis's encroaching army as Henry retreated. But the war was lost.

A showdown ensued between the two men. De Montfort compared Henry to Charles the Simple, a notoriously weak Carolingian king who had once paid off Rollo the Viking by making him Duke of Normandy. Henry was incensed but could say little in reply: de Montfort's charges contained a wounding truth. The failure of Poitou cost Henry £80,000 and bitter humiliation. Now Henry had to decide whether to have de Montfort executed for his treasonous words.

Perhaps surprisingly after the disaster of Poitou, Henry decided to reward de Montfort rather than punish him. He gifted the earl Kenilworth Castle and suggested he

WESTMINSTER ABBEY

HENRY INVESTED HEAVILY IN religious buildings such as Westminster Abbey, which he dedicated to the Saxon king, Edward the Confessor. Henry felt a great affinity for Edward as the only English king to be canonized.

With its gothic arches, marbled floors and great stained-glass windows, Westminster Abbey was a grand statement of Henry's power and piety. Future kings would be crowned, married and buried at Westminster; royal weddings still take place there today. It cost a fortune to build and decorate: some estimates put the final bill at around £50,000, more than twice the king's annual income.

Started in 1245, Westminster Abbey became Henry's life work; the barons complained about the cost of church processions and wax candles. They were horrified when the king bought a vial of what was said to be Christ's blood. The relic's authenticity had been attested by bishops in the Holy Land, and the treasure was smuggled under tight security into England.

Henry turned the entombment of the blood into Westminster Abbey into a solemn public show. The king stayed up all night to pray, before dressing in a simple cloak and receiving the vial and a host of priests at St Paul's Cathedral.

A procession of hooded churchmen carrying torches and crosses walked to Westminster Abbey in the cold autumn dawn. Henry led the way, carrying the vial above his head and continuing to stare at it during the ceremony. At the Abbey, Henry threw off his simple cloak to reveal an ornate robe of gold thread. The vial was then stored in a shrine intended to impress a multitude of pilgrims. But they never came. Even in the age of belief, few thought blood could last 13 centuries, even that belonging to Christ. Rumours soon started that the vial was actually filled with saffron and honey; others said it was simply refilled every week with goose blood.

Above: Henry is shown overseeing the construction of one of his many religious buildings.

become the king's lieutenant in Gascony, the last surviving Plantagenet region in France. In truth, Henry needed de Montfort to sort out a recent rebellion there; Kenilworth was to sweeten the deal. But Henry would later regret his decision to bring de Montfort back into the royal fold.

Henry was in an enlisting mood at this time. While de Montfort departed for France, the king invited a large number of his Lusignan cousins from Poitou. Once in England, the Lusignans were given titles and large estates, often confiscated from the English barons. French was still the official language of the court at this time, but courtiers who did not also speak English were frequently derided by the native nobility. Now that France was no longer part of the king's domain, a fervent nationalism was building in England and with it an increasingly open dislike of foreigners.

Below: Henry greets his wife, Eleanor of Provence, after her Savoyard retinue had been pelted by rotten eggs and vegetables by the Londoners.

This xenophobia had arisen in the 1230s when Henry had invited some of his wife Eleanor's uncles, the Savoyards, to act as his advisers. However, these were only some of the newest French arrivals. Henry's former regent Peter des Roches was French; Henry's mother was too. Simon de Montfort was of course French, but managed to avoid being stigmatized; as a long-term foreigner he was more acceptable to the xenophobes. De Montfort, however, hated the new Lusignan influx. The Savoyards hated them too. Most people did.

It could be considered an irony that Henry was so quick to invite the Lusignans into his kingdom if it weren't so typical of his behaviour. When the Lusignans had departed en masse from Poitou, the French couldn't believe their luck. Simply put, the Lusignans were a bad bunch: arrogant, violent and always spoiling for a fight. They soon broke into the Archbishop of Canterbury's Lambeth Palace, for no discernible cause, and ransacked it. They took the palace's treasure and hostages back to Farnham Castle to be ransomed. None were punished by Henry for these crimes.

> A FERVENT NATIONALISM WAS BUILDING IN ENGLAND AND WITH IT AN INCREASINGLY OPEN DISLIKE OF FOREIGNERS.

The problem for Henry was that the Lusignans provided muscle and money when he needed it. He was willing to overlook a bit of violence from these helpful people. He even ordered that the Lusignans couldn't be prosecuted. This was a serious blunder and directly contravened Magna Carta, which made it the sovereign's job to uphold impartial justice. The English barons complained directly to the pope, writing:

'If anyone brought a complaint and sought judgement against the Lusignans the king turned against the complainant in a most extraordinary manner, and he who should have been a propitious judge became a terrible enemy.'

Making enemies out of allies was Henry's speciality. There was no better example than when he recalled de Montfort from Gascony in 1248 after hearing reports that the earl was mistreating the local residents. He had, for example, cut the region's vines, a terrible punishment for grape-growers in wine country. Henry invited the Poitou complainants to London to present their case against de Montfort in front of a royal council, much to de Montfort's surprise. During the proceedings, a famous exchange took place between de Montfort and Henry, which was recorded by the monk, Matthew Paris.

'Who can believe that you are a Christian? Have you ever been to confession?' de Montfort demanded of Henry.

'Indeed I have,' Henry retorted.

'What is the point of confession without penance and atonement?' de Montfort shot back.

As with the couple's last exchange after the failed campaign in Poitou, de Montfort's words struck deep. Few at court that day would have disagreed with de Montfort's assessment, for it was the truth about Henry. Simply, the king never learned. He repeated the same mistakes over and over again, vainly hoping they would bring a different outcome. What happened next was another example of this, as it became clear that the royal council supported de Montfort and not Henry.

A wiser man would have accepted the council's decision, which ruled in de Montfort's favour. But instead Henry overturned the guilty verdict that was found against de Montfort.

Above: Henry III is confronted in Westminster Hall by his bishops over the threat of papal excommunication.

He then settled on a confusing compromise that involved paying de Montfort to resign his post and then travelling to Gascony himself to look into the matter. De Montfort was thunderstruck. There was nothing of their once great friendship left to salvage.

Henry stoked growing concerns about his competence when he set out a new scheme to expand his royal borders: an invasion of Sicily. This was originally the pope's idea. He suggested the king could invade the island under the papal banner and then install his son Edmund as monarch. It was not a new plan: the pope had offered the same deal to Henry's half-brother, Richard, the Earl of Cornwall, a few years earlier. Richard had immediately declined the offer by telling the pope's representative: 'You might as well say: "I will sell you the Moon, now climb up and take it."'

Henry, however, seized the proposal and told his assembled barons in 1255 that they should pay for it. More astonishingly still, Henry revealed that by agreeing to the Sicilian deal he would have to pay the new pope, Alexander IV, 135,541 marks, regardless of whether the expedition took place or not. It was a head-spinning sum and Henry did nothing to assuage the anger in the room when he presented his son Edmund, now apparently the incumbent king of Sicily, dressed in traditional Sicilian garb.

Breaking point was close. In 1257, the Welsh, led by Prince of Wales Llywelyn ap Gruffydd, attacked the English border. The same year the harvest in England failed, doubling the price of wheat and causing a countrywide famine. The chronicler Matthew Paris describes the scene in the villages of England: 'an innumerable multitude of poor people, swollen and rotting, lying by fives and sixes in pigsties or on dunghills or in the muddy streets.'

To add to the trouble, the hated Lusignans were now openly committing acts of violence against other nobles. This included the murder of a retainer of John FitzGeoffrey, a prominent nobleman. Henry, however, did nothing to rein the Lusignans in; he increasingly relied upon them for cash loans, especially with his new Sicilian debt. The king was also being threatened with excommunication if he defaulted. Henry's father John had put the country through six years of interdict, but this would not have been tolerated under Henry. His incompetence was now clear to all.

In 1258, a group of English barons in full battle gear marched into Westminster Hall and strode up to Henry's throne. Leading them was Simon de Montfort. 'What is this, my lords?' Henry asked. 'Am I to be your captive?' 'No, my lord,' replied Roger Bigod, the Earl of Norfolk. 'But let the wretched Poitevins [the Lusignans] and all aliens flee from your face and ours as from the face of a lion, and there will be glory to God in the heavens and in your land peace to men of good will.'

THE HATED LUSIGNANS WERE NOW OPENLY COMMITTING ACTS OF VIOLENCE AGAINST OTHER NOBLES.

The barons had left their swords at the door, but there could be no doubt that this was an ultimatum: accept our terms or risk violence. The barons then forced Henry to agree to a programme of constitutional reform that became known as the Provisions of Oxford. Only if the king shared power with an elected parliament would the barons agree to continue supporting him. The king had no choice but to agree – while also planning in secret how to renege on the deal.

Right: The barons confront Henry and force him to agree to the Provisions of Oxford.

THE PROVISIONS OF OXFORD

THE PROVISIONS OF OXFORD are widely considered to be the foundation of parliamentary democracy in England, and were issued in English as well as French and Latin, showing the growing importance of the language. England was increasingly aware of itself as a nation.

The Provisions were fairly simple: the king would share power with a 'Council of Fifteen' elected by 24 nobles, 12 picked by the king and 12 by the barons. The Council of Fifteen would meet in a parliament three times a year and as well as steering central government would investigate abuses of local officials such as the sheriffs. Four elected knights from every shire would hear complaints from ordinary people and make

sure they were presented to the justiciar. One such case was that of a local outlaw named Richard of Glaston who forced legal action after being assaulted by the Sheriff of Nottingham.

The Provisions of Oxford were hotly debated. The king's representatives were mainly made up of the Lusignans, who quickly become boisterous and threatening. Simon de Montfort called their bluff, saying unless the Lusignans handed back the English castles and lands gifted to them by Henry they would lose their heads. Sensing that the tide had finally turned against them, many of the Lusignans fled England for France. Perhaps the rats were deserting a sinking ship.

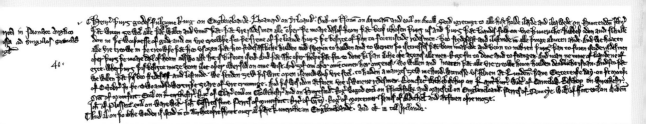

Above: A copy of the original Provisions of Oxford manuscript.

FOREIGN FORAYS

Henry lobbied the pope for divine help in avoiding his duties under the Provisions. In 1261, Pope Alexander absolved Henry from his oath and the king took up residence in the Tower of London, the great Norman symbol of power over England. Henry also began enlisting mercenary soldiers so he could reclaim the castles taken from the Lusignans and invite them back.

Simon de Montfort, meanwhile, had been under no illusion about Henry. In 1263, he denounced the king to the parliament for breaking his promise over the Provisions. Civil war was now imminent, with the country dividing quickly into rebel and royalist camps.

Many of the English barons had already been waging a propaganda war in the shires based on the slogan of 'England for the English'. Their so-called 'Second Barons' War' was ironically led by the Frenchman Simon de Montfort, who invaded London and set up his headquarters there. Henry in turn attacked the rebel town of Northampton while flying a red dragon with his royal standard, a sign that no quarter would be given. It was now only a matter of time before Henry and de Montfort came face to face in battle.

That great confrontation came on 14 May 1264 in Lewes, Sussex. De Montfort had little fear of Henry as a battlefield general, but Henry's son Edward was a different proposition.

Below: A 19th-century depiction of Henry III at the 1264 Battle of Lewes.

Tall, physically strong and
confident in arms, Edward
was more like his warlike
grandfather and great uncles
than his ineffectual father.
Edward lent pugnacity to the
king's side. He declared of de
Montfort and his rebels: 'Peace
is forbidden to them, unless
they all bind themselves with
halters on their necks and
hand themselves over to us for hanging
or drawing.'

Above: Henry III gifted the
mighty Kenilworth Castle
to Simon de Montfort,
only for it later to become
his prison.

Edward proved his prowess from the outset at Lewes, a
pitched battle on the Downs above the town. De Montfort
was badly outnumbered but held the higher ground. His 300
mounted knights looked down on a royal army of at least 1000
knights and a battle line that stretched out for nearly a mile in
front of them. Edward attacked the Londoners, a ragtag band of
amateur fighters who had once pelted his mother Eleanor with
rubbish in the capital. Edward had honed his fighting skills at
tournaments and now, in the manner of melee, he attacked the
Londoners and chased them across the Downs, maiming and
butchering as he went.

It was a classic beginner's mistake. Without Edward's soldiers,
Henry's army fell apart before de Montfort's battle-hardened
knights. By the time Edward rejoined the fray, Henry was
surrounded and the day was lost. De Montfort then debated
whether or not to behead the royalist leaders. He was persuaded
to be merciful, instead settling for a signed promise from Henry
to reinstate the Provisions of Oxford. Henry would remain king,
in name at least, imprisoned at Kenilworth Castle under de
Montfort's watch.

De Montfort met the king at Kenilworth and asked: 'What are
you afraid of? The storm has now passed over.' Henry replied:
'I fear thunder and lightning beyond measure; but, by God's head,
I fear you more than all the thunder and lightning in the world.'

For the next 15 months, Henry acted as a puppet king, rubber-stamping the policies of de Montfort and his parliament. In the meantime, however, a nationalist backlash was spreading throughout England. The country was still in the midst of its civil war, and chronicles of the time described the countryside being pillaged and burned by foreign mercenaries while worried

Above: Henry, dressed in Simon de Montfort's colours, is nearly killed by one of his son's knights.

watchers on England's white cliffs scanned the horizon for invaders. Matthew Paris, one of the most famous chroniclers of the time, was particularly xenophobic, praising one baron who fought to keep the country ethnically pure.

Behind the scenes, Prince Edward plotted his escape from Dover Castle. He succeeded by playing a game of 'find the fastest horse' while out riding one day with his jailors. Once he had found the fastest horse, Edward simply galloped away. Waiting in some nearby woods for him was the baron Roger de Mortimer, and together the pair rode off to raise another army.

At the Battle of Evesham in 1265, Edward faced de Montfort in a desperate attempt to revive Plantagenet power in England. This time, Edward positioned his army on the high ground, forcing de Montfort to ride up towards him from the town. As he did so a thunderstorm crashed, an ill portent of what was to come, as de Montfort could clearly see he was outnumbered. In an uncharacteristically defeatist moment, de Montfort was heard to remark: 'May the Lord have mercy upon our souls, as our bodies are theirs.'

If he was going down fighting, de Montfort was determined to take Henry down with him. He dressed the king in his own colours, which nearly had the desired effect, as Edward dispatched a squad of a dozen knights to seek out and kill de Montfort on the battlefield. Once the earl was gone, Edward was sure his army would crumble. Edward's knights very nearly slayed Henry by accident, but fate stayed their hand and they instead found de Montfort. The earl was already injured and was quickly finished off. The knights butchered the body, cutting off his hands and feet and hanging his severed testicles from his nose. De Montfort's head was sent for display in London.

It was the end of the rebel baron, but also more or less the end of Henry III. After Evesham, Henry became a feeble figure, spending his time praying and completing a new shrine at Westminster Abbey to his beloved Edward the Confessor before dying in 1272.

Under Henry the long road towards a parliamentary democracy had begun; so had a burgeoning sense of national identity. But did Henry ever think of himself as English? His last wishes for his burial are perhaps telling. He ordered his body to be buried at Westminster Abbey, but his heart to be put in Fontevraud Abbey alongside his kin. He was a Plantagenet to the last.

Below: Simon de Montfort is shown meeting his end at the 1265 Battle of Evesham.

4

EDWARD I & EDWARD II

Edward I and Edward II represent the two extremes of the Plantagenet personality. The first was a ferocious warrior king who invoked the spirit of Richard the Lionheart. The second was more like Henry III: pliable, indifferent and given more to gardening than fighting.

I N 1272, Prince Edward was in Sicily recovering from a knife wound when news came of Henry III's death. Edward had been waging an unsuccessful crusade in the Holy Land when a Saracen assassin bearing gifts duped his bodyguards and entered his bedchamber. The prince, who had been celebrating his 33rd birthday, awoke before the killer reached his bed. The struggle was described by the medieval historian the Templar of Tyre:

'The Saracen met him and stabbed him on the hip with a dagger, making a deep, dangerous wound. The Lord Edward felt himself struck, and he struck the Saracen a blow with his fist, on the temple, which knocked him senseless to the ground for a moment. Then, the Lord Edward caught up a dagger from the table which was in the chamber, and stabbed the Saracen in the head and killed him.'

— *LES GESTES DES CHIPROIS*, TEMPLAR OF TYRE

Opposite: Edward I presents his son, Edward II, the first English Prince of Wales, to the Welsh people.

Above: Eleanor of Castile valiantly sucks the assassin's poison from her husband's wound.

Opposite: Presiding over his parliament, Edward I is flanked by Scottish King Alexander III on his right, and the then Prince of Wales, Llywelyn ap Gruffydd, on his left.

Edward had escaped assassination, but the tip of the Saracen's blade was covered in a black toxin that caused the wound to fester. According to legend, Edward's wife, Eleanor of Castile, had immediately tried to suck the poison from the wound, but this did not stop the infection. A surgeon cut away Edward's rotting flesh and told him to recuperate in the warm Sicilian sunshine. But now there was news that would beckon Edward home: the king was dead; long live the king.

The chroniclers of Edward's time heaped praise upon the new king, or 'Longshanks' as he was known for his long limbs. Edward was six feet tall, and Matthew of Paris described him as of 'lofty stature, of great courage and daring beyond measure'. His penchant for warfare certainly made Edward popular with his subjects after the incompetent generalship of Henry III. Indeed, there seemed little of his father in the young man, except

estre mis en la main de louurier iusques a ce quil soit
repare. Lequel colier aussi ne pourra estre enrichy de
pierres ou daultres choses reserue les ymage qui pourra
estre garny au plaisir du cheualier. Et aussi ne pourra
estre ledit colier uendu engaige donne ne aliene pour
necessite ou cause quelconque que ce soit

Alexander Rex
Scotie

Lewellin
princeps
Wallie

for the inherited drooping eyelid. Edward instead was a warrior, a knight who was called the 'best lance in the world'.

There was also a darker side to Edward, which showed itself in the mutilations and thievery he committed as a youngster. Edward was born with the fierce Plantagenet temper. He was said to have once literally scared the dean of St Paul's Cathedral to death; the Archbishop of York apparently died of depression after a particularly savage telling-off. Edward also once punched a pageboy so hard at a wedding that he had to pay him a hefty cash gift in damages.

From the outset Edward made a great show of his power and status as a strongman. For his coronation in 1274, Edward and his knights rode dramatically into Westminster Abbey on horseback, their horses' hooves clattering on the marble floor. After the ceremony, Edward removed his crown and swore he would not wear it again until he had 'recovered the lands given away by my father to the earls, barons and knights of England and to the aliens.'

Above: A woodcut of
Edward I's coronation
with his archbishops
in attendance.

Edward would establish legitimate ownership of land through the courts and parliament; he reaffirmed his commitment to Magna Carta and promised to rid the land of corrupt judges. Unlike Henry III, Edward saw parliament not as a hindrance to his rule but as a useful mechanism for raising wartime taxes: he would call at least two parliaments a year to request such funds.

Edward was a warrior king who wanted to expand his borders. However, his aspirations for a bigger kingdom did not lie abroad, but closer to home. In the king's eyes, Wales and Scotland were a natural extension of England, and therefore belonged to him. By consolidating his rule of the whole of the island, Edward intended to create for himself a British empire.

Among those swearing fealty to Edward at his coronation was Alexander III of Scotland; notable for his absence was the Prince of Wales, Llywelyn ap Gruffydd. This was a deliberate snub by the Welshman, who had fought against Henry III during the Second Barons' War and had recently became betrothed to the late Simon de Montfort's daughter. Refusing to pay homage to the new English king was as good as a declaration of war, and Edward needed no better excuse to invade.

Wales had been for decades a thorn in the side of Plantagenet kings. It was also the supposed stronghold of Arthur, the mythical king who ruled over a united England. Edward aspired to match Arthur's accomplishment. Arthurian legend had never been more popular in Europe; the alleged tombs of Arthur and his queen, Guinevere, had been discovered beneath Glastonbury Abbey after it burned down in 1184. The find had so enthralled Edward that he travelled with his new wife on their honeymoon to pay tribute to the skeletons. According to legend, Arthur was supposed to come to the rescue of the Welsh if they were ever under attack; it seemed unlikely they would have any such luck as Edward marched his army over the border in 1277.

Above: The seal of Alexander III, the 13th-century King of Scotland.

It was a formidable force, over 150,000 strong, and supported by ships sailing around the Welsh coast from Kent and Sussex. This great army had been sanctioned and paid for by parliament, and was led by the best military minds in England. The logistics alone were impressive: hundreds of thousands of crossbow bolts had been made in England, warhorses were brought in from France, and wheat to feed the troops shipped from Ireland. Seeing what was before him, Llywelyn surrendered before a battle was fought; Edward's plan to cut off his grain supply had also helped concentrate his mind.

During the peace talks, Edward allowed Llywelyn to keep his title of Prince of Wales. But Llywelyn's brother Dafydd took offence at the rule Edward had imposed on Wales; the English, he argued, would crush Welsh culture. So war began again. In 1282, the brothers made a series of attacks on the Welsh castles of Edward's barons and the king reassembled his army in response.

CASTLE BUILDING

AFTER THE DEFEAT OF the Welsh, Edward introduced a programme of castle-building to prevent any future rebellion. Edward's castles would dominate the Welsh countryside as a constant reminder and symbol of English rule. Prominent among them were Harlech, Conwy and Caernarfon, each designed by master castle-builder James of Saint George. Caernarfon became the Welsh capital under Edward. It was built on the site of a former Roman fort, and the remains of Western Roman Emperor Magnus Maximus were supposedly discovered when the castle's foundations were being dug. Edward took this to be providential: Caernarfon was to be based on the mighty walls of Constantinople, capital of the Christian Roman Emperor Constantine.

To make it look like Constantinople, Caernarfon was built with many-angled towers and bands of multicoloured stonework running through its 6m (20ft) thick walls. It was deliberately imposing: a twin-towered gatehouse greeted visitors with a drawbridge, six portcullises and five gates. Punctuating the walls were a clever new invention: arrow slits. These were exactly the right size to fire an arrow from, but it was virtually impossible to get one through the other way.

Caernarfon took hundreds of workers five years to build and cost around £12,000, a heady sum in those days. While Caernarfon was being built, Edward's wife Eleanor visited the castle and gave birth there to their eldest son, Edward. Edward would be crowned Prince of Wales, the title previously held by Llywelyn ap Gruffydd. It has been tradition for the eldest son of the English monarch to be crowned the Prince of Wales since.

Left: Built to remind the Welsh of their English overlords, Caernarfon Castle was based on Roman Constantinople.

The conflict would drag on for nearly a year before its inevitable end. Llywelyn died in battle at the point of a lance and was then decapitated. Dafydd was betrayed by Welsh mercenaries fighting for Edward, captured at the small stronghold of Castell y Bere and sent to Shrewsbury for execution.

Edward would make an example of Dafydd: he was hanged until nearly dead and then disembowelled; his intestines were burned in front of him. His body was then quartered and a piece sent to four different English cities. Dafydd's head ended up on a pike in London, next to his brother's. Wales, the once independent nation of King Arthur, now belonged to the Plantagenets. To complete the humiliation, the crown of the Prince of Wales – said to have belonged to King Arthur himself – now rested on Edward's head.

NATION BUILDING

The conquest of Wales had shown Edward that to get things done he needed money and his barons' consent. Wales had meshed neatly with both: it had temporarily sated Edward's ambitions for expansion while giving his English subjects a cause they could support.

The growing sense of national pride could not now be reversed in England. There was little tolerance for unchristian foreigners such as the Jews. Jewish moneylenders had been seen as a necessary evil by many English nobles, including Edward himself. Their tenure in England, however, was becoming strained as increasing levels of xenophobia and anti-Semitism arose in the

Below: An illustration of Aaron of Colchester, a high-profile Jewish moneylender.

Below: A cartoon depicting the negative way Jews were viewed in England in the 13th century.

Below: One of three
remaining Eleanor crosses,
of which 12 were built by
Edward I in memory of
his wife.

late 13th century. During the 1270s, English hatred and mistrust of the Jews was such that the barons were willing to pay a tax to have them removed. After all, the barons would say, the Jews had been warned.

In 1279, Edward arrested and executed 300 Jewish leaders on charges of coin clipping; he then ordered all Jews in England to attend Christian sermons in the hope they would convert. They did not. In 1290, Edward formally announced his Edict of Expulsion of Jews from England, a community of between 2000 and 3000. In a sinister portent of modern events, a group of around 200 London Jews were made to wear yellow badges on their coats before being shipped down the River Thames. When they reached the river estuary the captain made his passengers disembark on a sandbar and then left them stranded as the tide rose. All of them drowned. Their property, left on the boat, was taken as a bonus by the captain.

The captain was jailed for this crime, but theft of Jewish property was also taking place in higher social echelons. Edward himself confiscated the goods and assets of many Jews he had expelled and pocketed the proceeds. A tax imposed on English subjects to remove the Jews earned him more than £100,000; Englishmen had to pay for their anti-Semitism.

Edward's taxes had long been an unsustainable burden on England. The barons would not pay for Edward to reinvade his Duchy of Gascony, recently taken by the new French king, Philip IV. The barons would, however, consider a war with Scotland.

Scotland was without a male heir since King Alexander III had fallen off his horse while galloping to spend the night with his new French bride. The choice for a new king lay between

John Balliol and Robert Bruce. Edward had been enlisted to help adjudicate this decision, which was known as the 'Great Cause'. It was a welcome distraction for the king: his wife Eleanor had died of a fever in 1290 and the king was beside himself with grief. He famously ordered a large stone cross to be put up at every point at which Eleanor's body had stopped on its journey from Nottinghamshire to London; a replica of an 'Eleanor Cross' still stands outside London's Charing Cross station.

Above: The Abbot of Arbroath delivers news to Edward that King of Scotland, John Balliol, had renounced his loyalty.

In the end, Edward chose John Balliol to be King of Scotland and immediately began treating him like a vassal. In 1294, Edward ordered Balliol to provide troops and arms to take back Gascony. This Balliol did, but behind his back a group of Scottish nobles began negotiating an alliance with France. When he learned of this, Balliol had little choice but to renounce his fealty to Edward.

In response, Edward marched his army to Scotland and swiftly overran the country's lowlands. He ransacked the trading port of Berwick-upon-Tweed and massacred the town's inhabitants, including women and children. The corpses were reportedly torn to pieces and thrown into the sea; more than 11,000 were killed in this way. In 1296, remaining Scottish resistance to Edward was defeated at the Battle of Dunbar. Balliol now surrendered to Edward.

A ceremony of public abasement took place. Edward ripped the royal red and gold insignia of Scotland from Balliol's coat (giving him the name 'Toom Tabard', or Empty Coat) and brought back to Westminster the Stone of Scone, upon which the Scottish kings were traditionally crowned. Edward then pronounced himself ruler of Scotland. As he did so, Edward handed the Seal of Scotland to his new English governor and remarked that 'a man does good business when he rids himself of a turd'. These humiliations would not stand for long with the Scottish leaders William Wallace and Robert Bruce; retaliation was coming.

WILLIAM WALLACE

A SMALL LANDOWNER BORN in 1270, William Wallace was a resistance fighter during the reign of Edward I and one of Scotland's greatest national heroes. He fought against the English during Edward's invasion in 1296, but managed to evade capture. He then waged a guerrilla war, leading a series of raids on English outposts.

The most prominent raid came in May 1297, when Wallace and around 30 of his followers attacked the town of Lanark and killed its English sheriff. Before long, Wallace had become the recognized figurehead for the Scottish rebellion against Edward. Under his command, Scottish soldiers utterly defeated the English at the 1297 Battle of Stirling Bridge.

The battle took place around the bridge, which was only wide enough to accommodate two soldiers across at a time. From a hiding point above, Wallace allowed around 2000 English soldiers across the bridge before his men descended upon them.

Those troops who were already across the bridge were slaughtered while others tried to turn back or ford the river. The result was a massacre of over 5000 English infantrymen and 100 knights. Stirling was a great victory for Wallace, who reportedly had the skin flayed off the body of English knight Hugh de Cressingham to make a scabbard for his sword. Wallace, named Guardian of Scotland by his followers, sent a message to Edward: 'Tell your commander that we are not here to make peace but to do battle, defend ourselves and liberate our kingdom.'

Left: William Wallace is one of Scotland's great national heroes and a pivotal figure in Scotland's struggle for independence against England.

THE BATTLE OF FALKIRK

After his victory at Stirling, Wallace retreated into the Highlands, destroying crops as he went to prevent them falling into the hands of the English. His strategy was to antagonize Edward and draw him into further military action on his turf. And that is what the king did.

Edward finally met Wallace face to face at the Battle of Falkirk in 1298. The fight began badly for Edward. He fell off his horse, which trampled him and broke some of his ribs. The king's supply train had been attacked several times en route and his men were now hungry. There had also been a fracas between the English knights and Welsh infantry, who were drunk, and 80 Welshmen had been killed. If morale was not low enough on 22 July, the day of battle, it was also raining.

Wallace had arranged his troops in front of Callendar Wood in round defensive formations called 'schiltroms'.

SUCH WAS HIS ENMITY TOWARDS THE SCOTS THAT EDWARD INSISTED THE FIGHT AGAINST THEM GO ON INTO ETERNITY.

Left: Here, the Bishop of Durham leads a charge at the 1298 Battle of Falkirk.

These had the appearance of hedgehogs, with spears and lances pointing outwards and archers at their centre. An early attempt by the English cavalry to smash through the front line of one schiltrom had shown its effectiveness: the formation held fast while dozens of knights perished at the end of enemy lances.

After this first action by the English, Wallace ordered his cavalry to charge. But when they saw the vast English army of 15,000 men – almost three times that of the Scottish – the cavalry fled the battlefield. The tide had turned. Edward ordered his archers to the front line before Wallace's schiltroms. Under a rain of arrows the schiltroms fell apart. Edward's infantry marched forward to mop up the stragglers. The Scots were defeated.

Wallace himself gave up his title of Guardian of Scotland after the Battle of Falkirk and was captured near Glasgow in 1305. He was condemned as a traitor and taken to London. There, he was dragged by horses from Westminster to Smithfield, where he was hanged until nearly dead. Then he was cut down, disembowelled, castrated and had his entrails burned before him. Finally, he was quartered and beheaded: his head was dipped in tar to preserve it and placed on a pike on London Bridge.

The fight for Scottish independence did not end with Wallace. In 1306, Robert Bruce became the movement's next leader. Infuriated by this news, Edward once again prepared to march on Scotland, telling his men garrisoned there to 'burn, destroy and waste' all that they saw before them. This led to atrocities against the Scots, which included having two Scottish noblewomen locked in cages and hung up for public view.

Despite Edward's rage, the king's race was run. On his journey to Scotland, now in a litter because of failing health, Edward died. His master plan to unite all of Britain into a

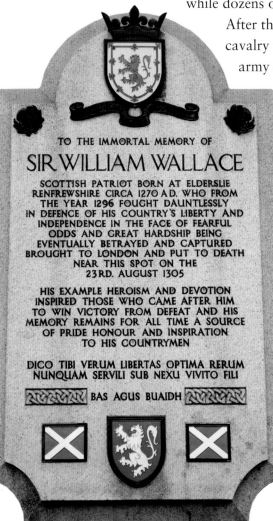

Above: This memorial to Sir William Wallace sits outside St. Bartholomew's Hospital, London.

Plantagenet empire had failed; he had been outdone by the Scottish. However, such was his enmity towards the Scots that Edward insisted the fight against them go on into eternity. Among his last orders was that in any subsequent campaign against the Scots, his bones should be disinterred and carried with the English army; he would continue to lead them even in death. This order was never carried out, but another of the king's dying wishes was. He ordered that his tomb would bear the name 'Edward I, Hammer of the Scots, Keeper of the Faith.'

Above: Edward I's body is carried by his men on its last march. His vision for a united Britain was stymied by the Scots.

Below: A portrait of the new Plantagenet king, Edward II.

EDWARD II

Edward II is often remembered for the violent and lurid description of his supposed murder, for he was not a well-liked king. He was weak-willed and uninterested in his kingship. Instead of ruling England, Edward preferred the company of close companions at court, and it was his relationship with them that defined his rule. This is how Edward was described by one contemporary chronicler:

'He was tall and strong, a handsome man with a fine figure...if only he had given to arms the attention he expended on rustic pursuits, he would have raised England on high; his name would have

resounded through the land. Oh what hopes he raised as Prince of Wales! All hope vanished when he became King of England! Piers Gaveston led the king astray...'
— *VITA EDWARDI SECUNDI*

Piers Gaveston was Edward's inseparable companion, brought to court from Gascony by Edward's mother Eleanor when the boys were teenagers. They were the same age, but Gaveston was a promising knight and it was hoped some of his military prowess would rub off on Edward. Instead, the couple enjoyed more frivolous pursuits: it is unclear whether their relationship was sexual but they were clearly infatuated with each other. It did not take long for Edward I to realize Gaveston exerted a bad influence on his son, and he was sent back to France.

In 1307, while Edward was out riding, news reached him that his father had died. It is telling that his first order as Edward II was to send word to France: tell Gaveston he is recalled to the royal court. This was typical of the king and his rule. His desires came first and the realm second. And in making decisions about these private matters Edward was blinkered to the point of blindness.

Below: Here, royal favourite Piers Gaveston leads Edward II astray.

THE ROYAL CORONATION

PIERS GAVESTON REACHED ENGLAND in time for Edward's 1308 coronation at Westminster. It was a farcical event. To start with, the Abbey became so overfilled with well-wishers that a dividing wall collapsed, killing one knight. The procession of dignitaries accompanying Edward and his 12-year-old bride, Isabella of France, to the altar was carefully choreographed to ensure the most important figures in the realm took priority. Many were astonished, therefore, to see Gaveston, dressed in robes of imperial purple decorated with pearls, at the head of the procession. He had also been given the privilege of carrying the crown and fixing a spur to the king's left foot. Gasps and cries went up at this breach of royal protocol.

The ceremony was only the beginning of a mounting scandal. At the banquet after the coronation, it was not Edward and Isabella's coats of arms that adorned the walls around the hall, but Edward and Gaveston's. During the feasting, Edward 'preferred the couch of Gaveston to that of his queen' and Isabella's family left early, indignant at the snub. To round off the day, Edward gave all his coronation presents to Gaveston.

Below: Edward II's 1308 coronation was a scandalous spectacle that often broke with royal protocol.

A few weeks after Gaveston had arrived, Edward made the shock announcement that he was making him Earl of Cornwall. The appointment raised alarm bells for the other barons. Cornwall was always reserved for royal family members, and the other barons hadn't been consulted over candidates. Worse still, there was not one baron in England who didn't openly despise Gaveston.

This hatred had been entirely of Gaveston's own making, as the earl always had a 'haughty and arrogant manner' at court. Gaveston had nicknames for all of the English barons, which included 'burst belly' for the Earl of Lincoln and 'black dog' for the Earl of Warwick. But Gaveston was about to find out that the dog could bite.

In 1308, a group of barons told Edward that unless Gaveston was exiled again there would be trouble. When the king refused, the barons returned two months later to make the same demand – but this time they were armed. They also had the backing of Edward's wife Isabella, his mother Eleanor and the Archbishop

Right: Piers Gaveston here walks past the English barons, who openly despised him.

of Canterbury. The archbishop threatened to excommunicate Gaveston if he was not sent away. In the end, there was little Edward could do. Gaveston was banished to Ireland.

As soon as Gaveston had departed, Edward appealed to the pope to overturn the order and overrule the threat from the archbishop to excommunicate the Earl of Cornwall. In the meantime, two other figures stepped into the gap left by Gaveston: Hugh Despenser the Elder and Hugh Despenser the Younger. Hugh Despenser the Elder was the only baron to argue against Gaveston's exile and would soon become Edward's leading adviser. Both Despensers would become as despised as Gaveston.

INERTIA AND BOTCHERY BECAME HALLMARKS OF EDWARD'S RULE.

In 1309, the pope did what Edward had asked and annulled Gaveston's exile. Within weeks Gaveston was back. It was a desperately shortsighted move by Edward, which alienated almost all of the barons. For them, Gaveston represented everything that was weak and decadent about the king. Edward was said to sleep late, delay making important decisions at all times, and even mismanage the finances of his personal household.

Inertia and botchery became hallmarks of Edward's rule. He failed to raise an army to deal with the increasingly pugnacious Scottish leader Richard Bruce, despite an emergency 25 per cent wartime tax on English subjects for just such occasions. Edward also carried out confiscations of land, breaking the terms of Magna Carta. There were rumours that the barons would soon take up arms against the king.

At the parliament of 1310, the barons presented Edward with an ultimatum: sign a list of 41 Ordinances or lose the crown. Edward, the barons explained, had not 'kept the oath he had taken at his coronation.'

The Ordinances gave a committee of 21 barons the power to rule the nation. They forbade the king from declaring war or leaving the country and all of his spending would be supervised. He would be hamstrung; a monarch only in name. It is a telling indication of Edward's priorities that he agreed to all of the Ordinances except article 20. This was a specific decree that

Gaveston was to be permanently exiled. The barons stood firm. Edward was forced to send Gaveston away once more.

This time, Edward waited a whole month before recalling Gaveston to England. He then sent public notices throughout the land rescinding his oath to the Ordinances and announcing that Gaveston had been restored to his earldom. It was a declaration of war against the barons.

Some of them went after Gaveston directly, seizing him at Scarborough Castle and placing him under the watch of the Earl of Pembroke. With his captive in tow, Pembroke travelled south to the town of Deddington. Oddly, Pembroke then decided to leave Gaveston under armed guard for one night while he visited his wife. But watching Gaveston was the man he had once derided as the 'black dog': the Earl of Warwick. And that night the black dog bit back, as the following account describes:

Below: Piers Gaveston is brought before Warwick, the earl he nicknamed 'the black dog'.

'When the Earl of Warwick had learned all that was happening about Piers [Gaveston], he took a strong force, raised the whole countryside and secretly approached the place where he knew Piers to be. Coming to the village very early in the morning one Saturday he entered the gate of the courtyard and surrounded the chamber. Then the earl called out in a loud voice: "Arise traitor, thou art taken." And Piers, hearing the earl, also seeing the earl's superior force and that the guard to which he had been allotted was not resisting, put on his clothes and came down from the chamber. In this fashion Piers is taken and is led forth not as an earl but as thief; and he who used to ride palfreys is now forced to go on foot…now Piers has laid aside his belt of knighthood, he travels to Warwick like a thief and traitor, and coming there he is thrown into prison. He who Piers called Warwick the Dog has now bound Piers with his chains.'

— *VITA EDWARDI SECUNDI*

Below: Gaveston's head is presented to the barons. His body lay where it fell until some monks retrieved it.

At Warwick, Gaveston was tried before a kangaroo court of hostile barons and sentenced to death as a traitor. As he was led from his cell at Warwick, Gaveston was said to have thrown himself to the ground, crying and pleading with the Earl of Lancaster to save him. But the earl was unmoved, saying: 'Lift him up, lift him up. In God's name let him be taken away.'

Gaveston was taken to a place called Blacklow Hill, where he was run through with a lance and beheaded. His body lay unburied until two Dominican friars retrieved it and sewed the

THE BATTLE OF BANNOCKBURN

THE ARMY EDWARD MARCHED to Scotland to put down Robert Bruce was the largest raised in England for well over a decade. It included 2000 cavalry, 25,000 infantry and a supply train of carts 32km (20 miles) long. Conspicuous by their absence were the earls of Lancaster and Warwick, who said they were not obliged to fight. Secretly they wished for Edward to fail, in case in victory he then turned his army on them.

Edward's army met Bruce's inferior force of around 500 cavalry and 6000 infantry at a boggy piece of floodland called the Bannock Burn. To make the terrain more treacherous for the English cavalry, the Scots had dug small pits to break up their charge. The battle began when Robert Bruce split the skull of English knight Henry de Bohun, who had charged at him on horseback.

The English cavalry then charged at the Scottish infantry, but their line was easily broken by the 4.5m (15ft)-long Scottish spears that protruded from their schiltrom formations. The English beat a hasty retreat before the day turned into a massacre. This would be postponed for the next morning.

The next day, the demoralized English cavalry prepared once again to attack and once again, many met their end at spear point. Others of the English cavalry were forced to dismount on to the boggy ground and a muddy, chaotic melee broke out. The English knights were soon caught between the Scottish schiltroms and their own advancing infantry; many died from friendly arrow fire.

When Robert Bruce unleashed his own cavalry on to the battlefield a cry went up among the Scots: 'On them! On them! They fail'. Edward and 500 of his closest retainers fled the battlefield and then Scotland, leaving thousands of Englishmen to be slaughtered. It was a terrible defeat and one that seemed to send a shattering message: Scotland would never belong to England.

head back on. Gaveston was not buried until 1315 when his papal excommunication was lifted. The most despised man in England was gone. Edward was beside himself at the news. He promised revenge, especially on the Earl of Lancaster, whom he viewed as the main perpetrator of the crime. Gaveston had not been tried in a legitimate court and his murder had therefore been a criminal act; however a compromise had to be made to avoid civil war. In the end an uneasy truce was made between Edward and Ordainers, and the king resumed his rule.

Above: The 1314 Battle of Bannockburn was a rout for the Scottish who left thousands of their English foes massacred on the battlefield.

Below: Robert Bruce
was the king who freed
Scotland from England
and cemented its
independence.

Everyone needed Edward as monarch now, as the rebellious Robert Bruce had besieged Stirling Castle and demanded its surrender. War with Scotland was at hand.

Edward faced humiliation and an immediate dissolution of his powers when he returned to England. After the failure of Bannockburn the Earl of Lancaster insisted Edward be bound by the Ordinances. Defeated and alone, Edward agreed. 'The king granted their execution and denied the earls nothing,' said one chronicle.

From that point on, England was split into two baronial factions: those for Edward and those against. Perhaps predictably, civil war broke out in 1321 when the factions fell out with each other. In the war, Edward's enemies were led by the Earl of Lancaster, and the royalists by Hugh Despenser the Elder. Both men were greedy, power-hungry and incompetent.

The Despensers would now show their true colours. Hugh Despenser the Younger was made the king's chamberlain and began seizing land and castles in Wales under the pretext of putting down rebellions for the king. The Despensers stole, extorted money and put those who protested on trial or simply murdered them. Edward remained complicit in the Despensers' misdeeds, concentrating his own efforts on finding a way to kill the Earl of Lancaster in revenge for the murder of Gaveston.

Hugh Despenser the Younger soon took the place of Gaveston as Edward's constant companion and the most despised figure in England. To protest against the Despensers and force a reconciliation, Lancaster and his barons marched on Westminster in 1322 and demand that the pair be banished. Queen Isabella fell on one knee and begged her husband to agree. This Edward did, but then recalled the Despensers shortly afterwards to raise an army against Lancaster. Lancaster had been found guilty of treason. Intercepted letters between Lancaster and Robert Bruce left no doubt that Lancaster had betrayed the throne.

Lancaster was subsequently beaten in battle by the Despensers and summarily beheaded. It took three blows of a sword to do this, as Edward himself watched on eagerly. With Lancaster dead, Edward could force the repeal of the Ordinances: the king and the Despensers were now off the leash. Edward immediately ordered the execution of 25 of his barons and the imprisonment of several others, included Roger Mortimer of Wigmore. 'Oh calamity,' recorded the chronicle *Vita Edwardi Secundi*, 'to see men lately clothed in purple and fine linen appear now in rags and bound up in shackles.' The bodies of those executed were hung in gibbets and left to decay.

Below: The Earl of Lancaster is taken to his execution after leading the baronial rebellion against Edward.

Edward's purge was carried out partly in public. Behind the scenes, he allowed the Despensers to begin a campaign of terrorism, including threatening to burn the widows of barons unless they relinquished their lands.

The Despensers refused to return Isabella's castles at Marlborough and Devizes captured during the civil war. They then confiscated all of Isabella's lands in England. As a final blow, Hugh Despenser took Isabella's youngest children into his custody for their 'own protection'. Edward looked on ineffectually as Isabella fled the country for Paris in 1325. Here, she felt she would be safe at the court of her recently crowned brother, Charles IV.

Below: Isabella arrives at the court of her brother Charles IV. From Paris, Isabella would plot her revenge against the 'Pharisee'.

THE SHE-WOLF'S REVENGE

Once in Paris, Isabella announced that she would not return to England and that her marriage to Edward was suspended. She told the French court:

'I feel that marriage is a joining together of man and woman, maintaining the undivided habit of life, and that someone has come between my husband and myself trying to break this bond. I protest that I will not return until this intruder is removed, but discarding my marriage garment, shall assume the robes of widowhood and mourning until I am avenged of this Pharisee.'

— *VITA EDWARDI SECUNDI*

Isabella intended to get her revenge on Hugh Despenser the Younger; he would have done well not to underestimate the queen known to history as the 'She-wolf of France'. Despenser had become everything to Edward that Piers Gaveston had once been. It was impossible to have an audience with the king without Despenser being present. But the country was descending into anarchy under the couple's rule: criminal gangs were terrorizing English shires and corrupt sheriffs were doing little to bring them to heel. The power of the barons to take control had diminished after the execution of the Earl of Lancaster: many in England now feared for their lives.

> HUGH DESPENSER WOULD HAVE DONE WELL NOT TO UNDERESTIMATE THE QUEEN KNOWN TO HISTORY AS THE 'SHE-WOLF OF FRANCE'.

The baron who would change the fate of the country, however, had escaped. Roger Mortimer, locked up in the Tower of London by Edward, escaped in 1323. This was famously done during the feast of St Peter ad Vincula, when Mortimer had managed to drug the wine of his captors. He broke a hole in his cell wall using a crowbar and scaled down the castle walls on a rope ladder to the River Thames. He then sailed directly to Paris and the bedchamber of Isabella.

It is unclear if Mortimer and Isabella had previously been lovers in England but in France the union quickly became public knowledge. The news of their intrigue became one of the great royal scandals of the day and rumours soon flowed that

Mortimer and Isabella were raising an army to attack England and kill Hugh Despenser. In September 1326, this is just what the couple set out to do.

The force of around 1500 soldiers that Isabella and Mortimer assembled was too small to be considered an invasion threat to Edward. However, as the army landed in Suffolk, it grew exponentially as recruits flocked to join. Isabella sent out letters offering a reward to anyone who brought her the head of Hugh Despenser. Edward and Hugh Despenser fled the Tower

Below: Roger Mortimer escapes the Tower of London after stupefying his captors with wine.

of London and escaped west. Londoners rose in revolt against the hated John Marshal and Bishop of Exeter, allies of the Despensers. Both men were killed, mutilated and decapitated with a knife.

Hugh Despenser the Elder tried to evade capture by barricading himself in at Bristol Castle, but the castle was besieged by Isabella's army and the earl imprisoned. He was then drawn, quartered and beheaded and his head sent for public display in London.

His son's fate was rather different. Edward and Hugh Despenser the Younger had travelled to the castle of Caerphilly in Wales. They could have held Caerphilly against a besieging army for some time, but they left after hearing a squad had been dispatched to hunt them down. They were captured trying to outrun their mounted pursuers on foot in a forest near the castle. Almost all their retainers had deserted.

Hugh Despenser was taken to Reading Castle, where it was reported he refused food and water in an attempt to starve himself to death before his impending execution. He failed, and was executed in front of a large crowd including Roger Mortimer and Isabella. Isabella was reported to have eaten throughout the proceedings.

DESPENSER WAS HUNG FROM A LADDER UNTIL NEARLY DEAD BEFORE HIS GENITALS WERE SLICED OFF AND FED TO A FIRE BELOW HIM.

Despenser was led before the crowd on horseback wearing a crown of thorns. He was quickly unhorsed by onlookers, who dragged him to the ground and cut biblical words into his skin with knives. To the sound of drums, Despenser was then hung from a tall ladder until he was nearly dead before his genitals were sliced off and fed to a fire below him. His heart and entrails were also cut out and thrown into the fire; it was then that for the first and last time he was said to utter a cry. His body was quartered and the pieces sent around the country in the traditional manner.

Edward himself was jailed in Kenilworth Castle. Under orders from an assembly of barons and bishops he was forced to abdicate in favour of his son Edward in return for his life.

Right: The brutal
execution of Despenser
took place on a tall
ladder so all could see.
Isabella ate throughout
the proceedings.

The 'father of the king' would live out his days in a small room
in Berkeley Castle, Gloucestershire. Edward received a generous
£5 per diem as an income, although there are conflicting reports
about how well he was treated.

Early in the morning of 23 September 1327, Edward III was
woken to be told his father had died. His death was from natural
causes, it was said, but soon rumours spread that he had been
murdered by Isabella and Mortimer. There are no verifiable
reports of what happened, but one account said Edward had
been murdered by having a red hot poker inserted into his rectum
via a steel tube. It is more likely that he was suffocated, but
neither method left any identifiable marks as he lay in his coffin.
There are no surprises as to which version of Edward's murder
captured the public's imagination, both then and now.

Edward was buried at St Peter's Abbey in Gloucester and the
Articles of Deposition remains a reasonable summary of his rule:

'Throughout his reign he has not been willing to listen to good counsel nor adopt it...he has stripped his realm, and done all that he could to ruin his realm and his people, and what is worse, by his cruelty and lack of character he has shown himself incorrigible without hope of amendment.'

Below: Edward II being dragged to his supposed death by hot poker. In reality, no-one can be sure how he died.

EDWARDVS   III·

5

EDWARD III

Edward III was a warring king who united a broken England under a banner of chivalry and St George. But his reign was soaked in blood. Edward's dynastic ambitions led to industrial-scale slaughter against France; at home, the Black Death ravaged his kingdom.

E DWARD WAS crowned at the age of 14 in 1327 after his father's death. Edward II's corrupt rule had brought England to the brink, but now he was gone. Desperate subjects looked hopefully to the new teenage king and his royal regents Isabella and Roger Mortimer for stability and control. It would not be forthcoming.

Roger Mortimer, like many men suddenly granted great power, turned out to be as corrupt as his predecessors. He enriched himself with the lands confiscated from Hugh Despenser rather than return them to their owners. He then awarded himself with the title Earl of March, securing his place in the upper echelons of the English aristocracy. Mortimer, accompanied by Edward III, attempted to quell an uprising by Robert Bruce in Scotland. The campaign ended in such disaster

Opposite: Edward III was the 14-year-old who it was hoped would unite a fractured England.

that Mortimer had to renounce England's position as overlord of Scotland and pawn the crown jewels to settle the peace treaty with Bruce. Edward wept with anger at this outcome.

It is reasonable to assume Mortimer was behind the murder of Edward's father, Edward II. Many people in England believed this to be so, and it is hard to imagine the thought had not also occurred to Edward. Either way, Edward had decided Mortimer had to go.

In the cold, early hours of 19 October 1330, a group of 20 heavily armed soldiers crept along a secret passageway with a winding spiral staircase leading to Nottingham Castle. In their chambers above the group were Roger Mortimer and Isabella. Leading the soldiers was William Montagu, a 29-year-old knight and fierce companion of Edward. Montagu had told Edward that it was 'better to eat the dog, than be eaten by the dog' when discussing Mortimer.

Spare keys to the secret passage and royal chambers had been stolen by those loyal to Edward; now they were used to illegally enter the castle. The group burst into Mortimer's apartment and dispatched the household steward. Mortimer ran for his sword but was tackled to the ground and then bound. Witnessing the commotion, Isabella ran for the door while shrieking 'Have pity on noble Mortimer!'

Right: With a handful of retainers at his side, Edward snuck into Nottingham Castle to catch and arrest Roger Mortimer.

There would be no pity for Mortimer. He was sent to London and imprisoned in the Tower of London as he had been under Edward II. This time he would not escape to rejoin Isabella. Mortimer was tried, found to be a traitor and on 29 October marched through the capital to Tyburn where he was hanged and quartered without ceremony. The next month, Edward issued a proclamation that he was assuming full authority of the country as king – he was 18 years old.

ENTER EDWARD

Edward seemed capable of uniting a fractured and desperate country. Unlike his father, he was an approachable and engaging personality. He was tall, with penetrating eyes and a mane of golden-red Plantagenet hair. His wife Philippa, who had 'deep brown eyes' and was of 'fair carriage', bore Edward 13 children. She was said to be a steadying hand, despite the king's many infidelities.

Edward excelled in hunting, falconry and the knightly arts, and was fascinated with Arthurian legend. The Plantagenets had of course an ongoing love affair with the tales of King Arthur since the time of Henry II. Henry's wife, Eleanor of Aquitaine, had been responsible for fostering all things Arthurian at the royal court; romantic texts about Lancelot and Guinevere, Gawain the Green Knight and the quest for the Holy Grail followed.

Edward also aimed to serve the Arthurian code. Chivalry fused military and Christian ethics: it demanded knights be bold, devoted to their ladies and loyal to their liege. Edward used it as a way of binding his nobles and his subjects to the crown.

Below: Windsor Castle was designed to be Edward's Camelot. The designs for its keep and walls are shown here.

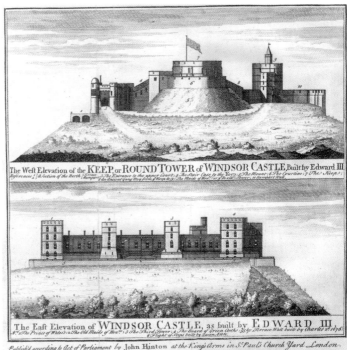

The West Elevation of the KEEP or ROUND TOWER of WINDSOR CASTLE, Built by Edward III

The East Elevation of WINDSOR CASTLE, as built by EDWARD III.

Publish'd according to Act of Parliament by John Hinton at the King's Arms in St Paul's Church Yard London.

The court was based at Windsor, a simple fortified castle that Edward built into a great palace. It would become the single biggest building site in England and was not completed until the time of George IV. Windsor's central quadrangle became a venue for lavish Arthurian tournaments. Edward was described in these early years as leading 'a gay life in jousts and tournaments

ROUND TABLES

In 1344, Edward III hosted the first of many Arthurian tournaments at Windsor known as Round Tables. The Round Table itself was represented by a round pavilion, on which the members of the order hung shields bearing their coats of arms. Those wishing to challenge a knight inside would do so by striking his shield. The ensuing joust between the knights would be watched by judges, ladies and other spectators from the nearby stands decked out in brightly coloured flags and banners.

The system of heraldry, or displaying one's colours, became increasingly complicated because there were so many coats of arms in circulation. It fell to the tournament heralds to identify the different coats of arms and explain to the spectators who they were. Heralds were expected to be well educated in knightly family histories as well as the colours they flew and helped spectating ladies who had their eye on a particular jouster.

Court ladies were central to the idea of Edward's tournaments and served as inspiration for the jousting knights, who would wear their particular scarf into the fray. The knight who out-jousted all challengers was given their horses and a gold crown to present to his chosen lady-in-waiting. Sometimes, to the surprise of the crowd, the knight would turn out to be Edward himself, bearing an anonymous coat of arms to ensure a fair fight.

Below: Courtly ladies were the central inspiration for battling knights at medieval tournaments.

and entertaining ladies.' Windsor would be Edward's Camelot. However, the serious aim behind the frivolity of tournaments was to prepare knights for war. And war would become a defining feature of Edward III's reign.

THE WARRING KING

After the failure of Mortimer against the Scottish king Robert Bruce, Edward was burning to retake Scotland. His chance came after a group of English barons staged an invasion of Scotland to repossess the lands they had lost under Mortimer's truce. Although winning a decisive battle in 1332 and installing the puppet Edward Balliol as king, success would not prove lasting.

Edward marched his army to Scotland to reinstate Balliol in 1333, and met the Scottish forces under Archibald Douglas at Halidon Hill. An entry from a contemporary chronicle known as the Book of Pluscarden explains how the Scots hamstrung themselves from the outset:

'They [the Scots] marched towards the town with great display, in order of battle, and recklessly, stupidly and unadvisedly chose a battleground at Halidon Hill, where there was a marshy hollow between the two armies, and where a great downward slope, with some precipices, and then again a rise lay in front of the Scots.'
— *BOOK OF PLUSCARDEN*

Right: Robert Bruce meets Edward III in 1327. In 1328, Bruce would sign the Treaty of Edinburgh–Northampton to end the First War of Scottish Independence.

The English had learned from the Battle of Bannockburn the folly of cavalry charges against the Scottish schiltroms. Instead, Edward positioned three divisions of archers around the top of Halidon Hill and ordered them to loose their arrows on the schiltroms advancing towards them. The schiltroms did not stay in formation for long. As many Scottish warriors ran for their lives, Edward sent his cavalry in pursuit; the result was a massacre, not only of Scottish infantry but of many knights and nobles.

Right: The Battle of Halidon Hill ended in a devastating defeat for the Scots fighting under Archibald Douglas.

After Halidon, Edward apparently abandoned his chivalrous ideals and marched his army on a slash-and-burn campaign of the Scottish lowlands. Crops, villages and their local populations were razed and put to the sword in deliberate acts of terror. It would not have a lasting effect, although Balliol was temporarily reinstated to the throne. By 1338, the Scottish leader David II, with help from the French, took control of the country and Edward was forced once again to sign a truce.

France's alliance with Scotland was a major problem for Edward. The countries had sworn to protect each other from the English under the Auld Alliance of 1295 and the English king did not want to wage war on two fronts. For it was France and not Scotland that really interested the warring king.

Edward's opportunity for a French action came in 1328 when Charles IV died with no male heir. One of the several claimants to the throne, Charles' cousin Philip de Valois, was crowned Philip VI. Edward, however, felt he had an equal right to the kingdom through his mother, sister to the late king. It mattered little to Edward that by French Salic law a woman could not inherit the crown.

Above: David II of Scotland here shakes hands with Edward III to ratify their truce.

Edward's imagined claim on France was brought into sharper focus when Philip VI annexed the Plantagenet territory of Gascony in 1337. In a roundabout way, this would lead to the Hundred Years' War between France and England, a conflict fought intermittently until 1453. Before a full-blown war, however, came a series of lesser skirmishes.

The most notable gave Edward control of the English Channel after he defeated an invading French force in the naval Battle of Sluys. In July 1346, Edward launched a major offensive in Normandy. Edward told the world he was the rightful king of France, but his real aims were to replenish his coffers through war and to frighten Philip VI into returning his Plantagenet heritage.

Edward's force marched under the banner of St George and included about 15,000 soldiers. Over half of this number were archers, trained to fire an arrow up to 200m (656ft). Their sheer number would make the skies black with arrows above the battlefields in France. Edward's army included cavalry, infantry, engineers, miners and clerks: a war machine that would prove unstoppable as it rolled across the French countryside.

Edward had ordered his troops not to harass the local populations as they marched, or rob local churches. Only the real soldiers in the ranks took notice of this; the rest – criminals, illiterate peasants and others press-ganged into the infantry – slaughtered, raped and stole as they went.

At Caen, Edward agreed to ransack the town instead of the castle after some initial negotiations. The English left the corpses of over 2000 inhabitants piled up in the streets and then marched towards Paris. From the capital the smoke of burning towns raided by the English could be seen along the horizon. The French destroyed the bridges leading over the Seine and built barricades in preparation for street fighting. It never came.

Instead, Edward turned his army towards Flanders, where they were due to join forces with a large Flemish contingent. It was said Edward marched his army at such a pace that his soldiers complained their shoes had worn out. It was not fast enough, however, as when the English reached the rendezvous they found the Flemish had packed up and gone home.

THE BATTLE OF CRÉCY

Philip VI now marched his own army towards the English king. The two forces met at a pitched battle near Crécy on 26 August 1346. Edward was in a buoyant mood, riding the length of his front line and joking with his men alongside his son Edward, 'the black prince'. Edward III had arranged two lines of infantrymen at the front and flanked them with divisions of archers. The army's supply carts made a barrier around the archers to prevent them being overrun by cavalry charges.

The French force of around 25,000 easily outnumbered the English. The French were known for their formidable cavalry

> CHIVALRY FUSED MILITARY AND CHRISTIAN ETHICS: IT DEMANDED KNIGHTS BE BOLD, DEVOTED TO THEIR LADIES AND LOYAL TO THEIR LIEGE.

and Philip placed them in two lines behind a facing line of
crossbowmen. On the flanks were arranged divisions of the
French infantry.

Both sides had been hurling insults at each other for hours
when the order for battle went up in the late afternoon. As the
trumpets sounded and the war drums beat, a flock of crows flew
above the battlefield and the rain that had threatened all day
began pelting down. The Genoese crossbowmen in the French
ranks stepped forward a few paces, and then stepped forward
again. The English archers, in return, made one step forward
and began loosing their arrows.

Above: The armies of
Edward III (right) and
Philip VI come together
for the 1346 Battle
of Crécy.

The white-painted English arrows rained down upon the Genoese so thickly 'it seemed like snow'. The Italian crossbowmen, by comparison, were not close enough for their bolts to reach the English front line. When they saw the English arrows piercing the heads and limbs of their comrades, many cut their bowstrings and fled from the field. Seeing the deserters, Philip VI shouted: 'Slay these rascals, for they shall let and trouble us without reason.'

With his force crumbling, Philip VI desperately ordered a cavalry charge. But this too was brought down in a blizzard of English arrows. It was then that Edward unveiled his secret weapon, never seen before on a battlefield in France: cannons. These were large, unwieldy and hard to aim, but their psychological effect alone would have been worth their addition.

For thousands of French soldiers, Crécy was to be nothing less than a vision of hell, as flocks of arrows whistled into their ranks, men and horses screamed out in their death throes, and cannon fire crashed through them. The French knights fought to their end, wishing rather to suffer glory in death on the battlefield

Below: Edward's wife Philippa persuades him to spare the six Burghers of Calais, who offered their lives so their city would be spared.

than the humiliation of defeat afterwards. A division of Welsh infantrymen were dispatched among the French wounded to finish off the stragglers with knives. Defeat for the French was absolute: over 14,000 men were killed to around 200 of the English. After Crécy, England's army became the most feared in Europe.

THE BLACK DEATH

Edward III's son, Edward the Black Prince, won his spurs at the Battle of Crécy and was a great hope for the throne. However, the Black Prince died, like so many other Plantagenets, of dysentery, in 1376. Edward III and Edward the Black Prince had both shone at the 1356 Battle of Poitiers, which ended in the capture of the new French king, John II. Edward, however, never became King of France.

Crécy was the high-water mark for Edward in battle: there would

be many other victories, but none of them so comprehensive. The booty taken from France made Edward rich; when he returned to England in 1347 it was to much fanfare: France had been soundly thrashed and another Scottish uprising had been similarly put down. And then, disaster struck.

The Black Death, also known simply as the plague, originated in Asia in the 1330s before spreading through continental Europe. It reached London in 1348.

Above: Edward III greets his son, the Black Prince, after his resounding victory at Crécy.

The plague, or the bacterium *Yersinia pestis*, mainly consisted of the bubonic plague carried by fleas living on shipboard rats. But its variants, pneumonic plague and septicaemic plague, made the Black Death even more contagious by blood or human fluids; sneezing on someone was usually enough to spread the sickness.

The plague thrived in unsanitary and crowded conditions and the symptoms were horrific, black ulcerated sores in a victim's armpits and groins, sometimes weeping pus. An infected plague victim suffered aching limbs, vomiting and diarrhoea and usually only had days to live. The pestilence spread across England within weeks.

During the period from 1348 to 1351, between a third and a half of the population died of the plague. Some estimate the deaths at two million. Cemeteries overflowed; the dead lay unburied in the street. Church bells fell silent, fishing boats lay still in harbours and crops rotted in the fields. Foreign boats stayed away from English ports for fear of infection, although the plague was already rife in Europe.

Below: The effects of the Black Death did not discriminate between man or beast.

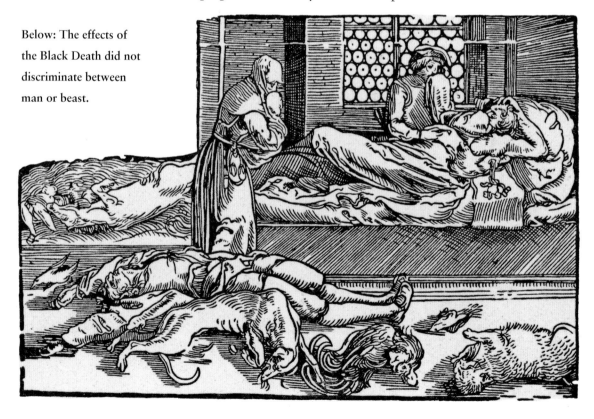

With so many labourers dead, landowners were forced to pay triple wages to bring in crops. Food was desperately short and land was sold off cheap to raise cash for wages. Parliament was not held in 1349, although Edward ordered labourers to stay in their own villages rather than travel to neighbouring shires for higher pay. Few paid any attention to this.

Edward himself lost two of his daughters to the Black Death: plagues paid no heed to rank or privilege. As the plague receded, Edward went ahead with plans to bring in an Order of the Garter to reward the most outstanding knights who had fought at Crécy. To be honoured every year on 23 April, St George's Day, the Order's inaugural meeting was celebrated with a tournament at Windsor. To be a member of the Order remains one of the highest honours in England today.

Below: The badge of the Order of the Garter. Membership of the order remains one of England's highest honours today.

The Order of the Garter's inauguration displayed all the pageantry expected of one of Edward's tournaments, but perhaps some of the colour had faded for the king. The massacre at Crécy had raised troubling questions about the concept of chivalry in war. For this reason, Edward abandoned plans to build an actual round table in Arthur's honour when he returned to England from France. Perhaps chivalry was best confined to romances and the fantastic past.

Chivalry had helped encourage Edward's subjects to go to war abroad. Over 200 years before, the Plantagenets had come to England as dynastic rulers taking overlordship of one of their possessions. They spoke only French and were not interested in the country's common tongue. But before he died in 1377, Edward passed the Statute of Pleading, formally making English and not French the official language of the law courts and parliament.

English was no longer just for the peasants, but the knights, nobles and sovereigns of England. It bound all future Plantagenet kings to the land and made them think of the country not as a possession, but an English empire.

6

RICHARD II

Richard II believed in his right to rule as God's appointed king. But his tyrannical reign ended in murder, rebellion and royal bloodletting. Many English kings would later also be subject to violent death at the hands of their own family. The Plantagenets would never recover.

O N 13 June 1381, Richard II watched anxiously from a turret in the Tower of London as an angry mob of peasants, armed with sticks, bows, axes and knives, ransacked the city below. Supportive Londoners had opened the gates to the city and the mob had streamed over London Bridge and poured into the capital unopposed. There they fell into a frenzy of destruction and murder: they burned down Duke of Lancaster John of Gaunt's Savoy Palace and killed his officials; ransacked the Temple, home to the city's lawyers; attacked the Fleet Prison and freed the inmates; and crossed the river to raze the Archbishop of Canterbury's Lambeth Palace.

The rebels destroyed property and looted as they went; many became drunk on stolen wine. For Richard and his royal retinue cowering in the Tower, the sight was terrifying. Smoke rose from

Opposite: This over-sized portrait of Richard II was designed to look down on English subjects from a great height, as the king did in person.

numerous buildings and the terrible din of destruction echoed across the city. The chronicler Thomas Walsingham noted that the rebels' shrieking and howling sounded as if the devil and all the inhabitants of hell had joined them.

All eyes turned to Richard, the 14-year-old king, for a solution. The rebels harboured no ill-intent towards Richard, or his cousin, the teenager Henry Bolingbroke, who had also taken refuge in the tower. Instead, the mob wanted the blood of the 'traitors': the chancellor and Archbishop of Canterbury, Simon Sudbury; the treasurer and prior of the Knights Hospitaller Robert Hales; and John of Gaunt, the Duke of Lancaster, Richard's uncle and Bolingbroke's father.

These men were the councillors of the young king who had introduced a new poll tax that had caused the riot. The tax had been imposed on every person in England over 14 regardless of their income. It had created a great outrage and for many peasants, breaking point. They had survived the recent

Right: Lollard priest John Ball tries to stir up rebellious sentiment among Wat Tyler and his followers during the 1381 Peasants' Revolt.

devastation of the Black Death and suffered the new labour laws restricting their rates of pay, but the poll tax and its collection of payment – often violently enforced by local sheriffs – had led to the uprising, later called the Peasants' Revolt.

The Peasants' Revolt was the largest rebellion of the working classes that had ever occurred in England; the rebels were over 30,000-strong. Now they stood before the Tower baying for the blood of those who had levied the taxes: 'Give us John of Gaunt!' the crowd chanted, 'Give us Sudbury!', 'Give us Hob the Robber!' (their name for Robert Hales).

Richard's councillors suggested that the young king parley with the rebelling peasants as a diversion – this would give them time to escape. Richard, believing he was under the protection of God, agreed to this. The king and his bodyguard rode to a field at Mile End to talk with a group of the rebels and their leader, Wat Tyler. After listening to Tyler's demands, Richard agreed to all of them. They amounted to little less than a complete overhaul of the social structure of England, including freedom from serfdom, the lifting of wage restrictions, and a free pass for the peasants to hunt down and kill the 'traitors'.

However, there would be few traitors left to punish. While Richard's meeting went on, rebels broke into the tower and butchered and beheaded Sudbury and Hale. Removing Sudbury's head had proved a particularly difficult task that required over eight blows to the neck; it left a terrible mess. The heads of the nobles were stuck on poles and paraded around London; they distinguished Sudbury by nailing his red bishop's mitre to his head. Henry Bolingbroke managed to evade capture by the mob after a quick-thinking knight hid him in a cupboard.

The murders seemed to re-energize the rebels. They stormed Westminster Abbey and seized the Marshalsea prison warden, who was hiding behind Edward the Confessor's shrine.

Above: Richard II here meets Wat Tyler's rebels in a miniature from Jean Froissart's *Chronicles*.

The warden was dragged to Cheapside and beheaded, alongside dozens of Flemish traders, and other foreigners and 'enemies'. The ground next to the makeshift chopping block became soaked in blood.

Meanwhile, Richard and his retinue took refuge in a bolthole at Blackfriars. In a last-ditch attempt to curb the rebels, Richard sent word that he wanted to talk to Tyler once more. Another meeting was arranged outside the city walls, in what is today's Smithfield meat market. This make-or-break moment would determine Richard's destiny as king – if he lived to tell the tale.

There was a tense, volatile atmosphere among the rebels waiting for Richard in the field beside the city walls. Richard presently rode up with a large guard who had concealed weapons

Below: Wat Tyler meets his end at the hand of Mayor of London William Walworth. The murder preceded a defining moment for the young Richard.

beneath their robes. Wat Tyler seemed drunk, on wine and his successes, and reiterated his demands from Mile End. These would have to be written down, signed and then enshrined into law before the peasants would disband, Tyler explained. Richard, as before, agreed that this would be done.

But suddenly a scuffle broke out between Tyler and the Mayor of London, William Walworth. Walworth drew his sword and delivered two blows to Tyler's neck and head: these would prove to be mortal wounds. Tyler turned to ride back towards his rebels, but fell from his horse before he reached them. A cry went up among the rebels, who began attaching arrows to their bows.

This was when Richard suddenly had a moment of regal inspiration. He galloped over to the rebels and called to them that he was king and leader and that under the eyes of God they must

> RICHARD'S DEMEANOUR WAS FROSTY AND ALOOF AND HE ADDRESSED THE PEASANTS IN COLD, CLIPPED TONES.

follow him. Incredibly, the speech worked. The rebels bowed their heads and many fell to one knee. As if to confirm the status and power of their lord, a group of royal horsemen rode on to the field ready to come to the king's aid. There would be no further bloodshed, however, and the peasants dispersed for home, believing they had won a great victory.

Richard's defining moment of bravery and majesty at Smithfield was a surprise to everyone there – except Richard. For since childhood, Richard had been told that God had appointed him to lead the people of England. During his coronation, Richard had been anointed with holy oil to confirm this. When the peasants knelt before him, therefore, it was simply further confirmation that the young king was fulfilling his divine destiny. There was never any danger, as God had protected him against the rebellious peasants.

However, Richard had no intention of remaining true to his promises. When a delegation of peasants visited the court 18 days later to discuss the details of the deal, they found an altogether different king. Richard's demeanour was frosty and aloof and he addressed the peasants in cold, clipped tones. It was a side of the king many would experience in the years to come. According to the chronicler Thomas Walsingham, this is what Richard said:

'You wretched men…who seek equality with lords are not worthy to live…Rustics you were and rustics you are still. You will remain in bondage, not as before but incomparably harsher. For as long as we live and, by God's grace, rule over this realm, we will strive with mind, strength and goods to suppress you so that the rigour of your servitude will be an example to posterity.'

– *HISTORIA ANGLICANA*, THOMAS WALSINGHAM

Below: The young Richard meets the peasants outside London's city walls, near today's Smithfield meat market.

With that, Richard set out to make good on his pledge – 150 of the rebel leaders were tried, found guilty of treason and executed, most beheaded. A parliament was then called to consider the question of serfdom and its potential abolition, lest it cause further uprisings. Both houses of parliament – the Commons and Lords – voted unanimously no to the motion: serfdom and the feudal system would remain intact. The Peasants' Revolt had ended in failure.

CLASS AND CLOTHES

SERFDOM WAS A FORM of bondage that bound serfs to a landowning lord. The serf would work on the lord's land in return for a small parcel of land to grow crops for their own subsistence. Serfs were not free to travel without permission, or move, or work elsewhere. Serfdom was the central tenet of Europe's feudal system, which placed the nobility and clergy at the top of the social hierarchy and the peasants at the bottom. By calling for an end to serfdom, the Peasants' Revolt was actually asking for an overhaul of the country's social and economic structure, so it is little wonder that the landowners in parliament would not agree – serfdom instead lasted well into the 16th century.

Some of the rules underlying the country's social structure were laid out in the 14th-century Sumptuary Laws. These divided the population into seven classes and decreed what each class was allowed to wear. One of the clauses in the 1363 Laws, for example, said: 'No knight under the estate of a lord, esquire or gentleman, nor any other person, shall wear any shoes or boots having spikes or points which exceed the length of two inches, under the forfeiture of forty pence.' In the same Laws were clauses for women, including: 'Wives and daughters of servants are not to wear veils above twelve pence in value'; 'The wife or daughter of a knight-bachelor is not to wear velvet' and 'Cloth of gold and purple silk are confined to women of the royal family'.

There were no restrictions on the dress of Richard himself, which was fortunate, for the king was a lover of fine clothes. Court fashions at this time included hosiery, doublets and codpieces for men, and bejewelled gowns and pointed shoes for women – the points were often so long they had to be attached to their garters for support.

1394.   DRESS 1386.   1399.

Above: Three 14th-century noblewomen model the popular styles of the day.

Above: Shown here in prayer, Richard II was fond of fine clothes and courtly extravagance.

Opposite: Richard II and his bride Anne of Bohemia are shown at the king's coronation. The marriage was said to be one of true affection.

COURTLY COMPANIONS

Richard was only a teenager, but his suppression of the Peasants' Revolt had shown his calculating, duplicitous side. He was quick to anger – as his Plantagenet genes dictated – and flushed and stammered when in a rage. This made Richard something of an *enfant terrible*: he was a tall, pretty man with high cheekbones, blond hair and large eyes; and once he had to be stopped after flying at the Archbishop of Canterbury with his sword drawn.

Richard's bride, the teenage Anne of Bohemia, was said to have a great calming effect on the king. Both loved the lavish lifestyle of the English court and often indulged in its ceremonies and spectacles. Richard was accused by one chronicler of living extravagantly and being less interested in fighting wars than in 'carousing with friends'. Finding wars to fight was considered, by many, to be one of the king's primary occupations. But instead of doing this, Richard favoured peaceful borders and a self-indulgent life at home. He showered lands and titles on his friends at court, a young guard of disreputable nobles that included Robert de Vere, Michael de la Pole and Robert Tresilian. The older nobles whose task was to advise the young king had a particular dislike of de la Pole, the low-born son of a wool merchant whom Richard had made Earl of Suffolk and chancellor. De la Pole's meteoric rise was unacceptable to the older peers at court.

The older nobles put pressure on Richard to assert the country's military might, as his father, the Black Prince, had once done so successfully. The war party included John of Gaunt, Duke of Lancaster; Thomas of Woodstock, Duke of Gloucester; and Richard FitzAlan, Earl of Arundel. Richard eventually assented to go to war – two botched campaigns followed in Flanders and Scotland.

The Flanders 'crusade' was led by the Bishop of Norwich, Henry Despenser, and aimed to save the trading town from French occupation. Despenser's campaign, however, ended in

the slaughter of many innocent Flemish inhabitants and then an unsatisfactory peace treaty with the French. No territory was gained for England and Despenser was impeached by parliament upon his arrival back in the country. He wriggled out from beneath this charge in time to join Richard's 1385 campaign in Scotland. Many nobles joined the 18-year-old king on the march north. Its purpose was to rid Scotland of the French garrisons stationed there, which were a threat to England. However, when the English force arrived, no French or Scottish armies could be found. Nobody would show up to engage Richard in battle.

The older nobles urged Richard to seek out his foe apparently hiding out in the Scottish Highlands, but Richard declined. Encouraging guerrilla warfare in the barren, windswept Highlands was war without reward; Richard ordered the long march home. Instead of winning prestige and loot as a warrior king, Richard returned to England with nothing. He would now have to address the internal war being waged at his court.

By 1386, there was a long list of grievances against Richard. His military forays had been a calamity, the royal coffers were nearly empty and there were rumours that the French king, Charles VI, had raised an army to invade England. Singly, these issues may not have been enough to undermine Richard's kingship, but combined with his choice of royal appointments, they were.

Above: A statue of Michael de la Pole, the son of a wool merchant who was gifted with lands and titles by Richard.

The grievances were laid bare at the later-named 'Wonderful Parliament' of 1386, which opened with a request from de la Pole to raise taxes to defend England against Charles VI. The peers howled and demanded that de la Pole be removed from office and imprisoned on charges of incompetence and embezzlement. Richard flushed at this suggestion and stammered that he would not rid himself of as much as a kitchen hand at the behest of parliament.

It was then that the nobles FitzAlan and Woodstock reminded Richard of the fate of his great-grandfather Edward II. The implication was clear: bad kings could be rolled, and perhaps later killed in their beds. Richard was a great admirer of his predecessor Edward and had petitioned the pope to have him canonized. The memory of Edward's murder perhaps tempered Richard's rage.

The king had no choice but to submit to the restrictions laid down by the Wonderful Parliament, including the removal of de la Pole. Once this was done, the parliament created a commission to take over the role of chancellor, with Richard allowed no part in it. His powers as king had effectively been revoked. Parliament had never been so powerful, nor the powers of the 18-year-old Richard so weak. It was a humiliation he would never forgive.

While parliament conducted the business of rule, Richard left London on an eight-month tour of the country. Richard's 'gyration', as it was called, aimed to drum up support. Travelling with him were the hated de la Pole and de Vere. Richard ordered a group of the country's most senior judges be assembled and asked them whether the ordinances imposed upon him by the Wonderful Parliament had been legal.

Left: Richard addresses the Wonderful Parliament which had revoked his royal powers.

After several tense hours, the judges told Richard what he wanted to hear: the ordinances had not been legal and those who had imposed them on the king could be punished as traitors. His Chief Justice Robert Tresilian also decided that the Wonderful Parliament's conduct had been unlawful and treasonous.

In 1351, Edward III had enacted the Statute of Treason to more clearly define what treason was. This was after the earlier executions of Piers Gaveston, Hugh Despenser and Roger Mortimer had been made in its name. Edward tightened the definition, so the act of treason largely meant an actual or planned attack on the king or one of his family members.

But now treason again became vague and overarching – those trying to issue reforms in parliament or impeach a rogue earl, for example, could be considered traitors, and so could those curbing the king's powers. Most of the members of the Wonderful Parliament now faced the prospect of losing their titles, fortunes and heads if Richard so willed it. Nobles around the country called men to arms in fear of arrest. Civil war beckoned.

RICHARD HAD NO CHOICE BUT TO SIT AND WATCH AS HIS FRIENDS WERE HAULED AWAY TO BE HANGED OR BEHEADED.

The problem was that both Richard and the lords of the Wonderful Parliament believed the other to be guilty of treason. The lords appealed to Richard to rid himself of de Vere and de la Pole and became known as the Lords Appellant. They refused to meet Richard in person, for fear of reprisals, but assembled a force with Henry Bolingbroke at its head, freshly returned from a crusade.

Richard, in response, retreated to the Tower of London and tried to raise a royal army. This failed because all of the support was with the Lords Appellant. Worse was to follow. The Lords Appellant tried to hunt down and arrest de Vere, who was leading his own army to London to help Richard. Bolingbroke nearly caught de Vere en route and the former chancellor escaped only by throwing off his armour and jumping into the Thames, later escaping to France. Now unopposed, the Lords Appellant surrounded the Tower and the king was

caught. Richard would now have to appear before the new
'Merciless Parliament'.

Parliament had complete power at this point, but it made
it clear Richard would not be deposed. At its opening, the
parliamentarians entered wearing gold robes before dramatically
linking hands and advancing on the king. They then bowed
before him, before beginning the business of stripping away
his royal powers. What followed was a purge of Richard's
household, the young nobles who surrounded him, and the
judges who had conspired to redefine treason to suit the king.

The MPs found Chief Justice Robert Tresilian guilty of treason
and sentenced him to death. Many more followed during several
months of parliamentary revolt. Richard had no choice but to
sit and watch as his friends were hauled away to be hanged or
beheaded. It was a devastating humiliation for the king.

Below: Members of the
'Merciless Parliament' here
explain to Richard exactly
how his royal powers will
be stripped away.

THE DEATH OF TRESILIAN

THE EXTRAORDINARY ACCOUNT OF the capture, arrest and execution of Robert Tresilian is recounted here by the chronicler Thoman Favent:

'[Tresilian] had been located above the gutter of a certain house annexed to the wall of the palace, hiding among the roofs for the sake of watching the lords coming and going from parliament. However, when resolute soldiers had entered that house and looking around found no one, a certain knight with intent expression strode to the father of the house and pulled his head up by the hair, drawing his dagger, saying, "Show us where Tresilian is or your days are numbered." Immediately, the terrified father of the household said, "Behold the place where that man is positioned at this moment," and under a certain round table which was covered for deception with a tablecloth the unfortunate Tresilian, disguised as usual, was miraculously discovered. His tunic was made out of old russet, extending down to mid-shin, as if he were an old man, and he had a wiry and thick beard, and wore red boots with the soles of Joseph, looking more like a pilgrim or beggar than a king's justice.

...At length Tresilian was bound hand and foot to a hurdle, and along with a vast multitude of lords and commoners, horsemen and pedestrians, he was dragged from the back of horses through the city squares...And when he had come to the place of Calvary that he might be made defunct, he did not want to climb the stairs but goaded by sticks and whips that he might ascend, he said, "While I carry a certain something around me, I am not able to die." Immediately they stripped him and found particular instructions with particular signs depicted in them, in the manner of astronomical characters; and one depicted a demon's head, many others were inscribed with demons' names. With these taken away, he was hanged nude, and for greater certainty of his death his throat was cut.'

Left: A medieval miniature showing the execution of Robert Tresilian.

THE ADULT KING

After the purges of the Merciless Parliament, many expected Richard to retaliate, but he did not. Instead the king appeared to take a more mature and sensible approach to his rule. For a time, there was peace in Richard's kingdom and prosperity as the royal books were balanced under the new council of the chancellery.

In 1389, Richard turned 22 and announced that he would now rule on his own without a council of elders. There was little anyone could do: Richard was the king. Besides, his attitude since the Merciless Parliament, while perhaps becoming more regal, had also been reconciliatory; there had been little to complain about. For a further eight years, Richard ruled in this way. However, at the royal court some subtle changes were instigated.

The first concerned the royal address. Richard wanted to be called 'your highness' and 'royal majesty' and 'your high royal

Below: The Wilton Diptych shows the divinely anointed Richard watched over by the saints and the Virgin Mary.

Opposite: Richard II's marriage to Charles VI's seven-year-old daughter Isabelle was designed to promote a period of peace with France.

Below: The death of Anne of Bohemia was a bitter blow to Richard II: he had genuinely loved his queen.

presence'. These new terms of reverence exasperated many nobles, but they humoured the king. Richard, however, grew increasingly obsessed by his supposed superiority. He had been anointed with the holy oil as God's ruler; God was therefore his only lord.

Richard adopted the symbol of the White Hart as his personal emblem and assembled a new entourage of close followers, known as the 'affinity', who all wore the badge. The White Hart began to appear everywhere, including in a famous artwork he commissioned called the Wilton Diptych. In this, Richard is shown accepting the royal crown from God and a group of angels wearing the White Hart.

The White Hart was an emblem of Richard's love of ceremony and pageantry, and the Wilton Diptych a splendid symbol of Richard's patronage of the arts. But there was trouble beneath the splendour. Wearers of the White Hart badge seemed increasingly akin to a cult: only the true and faithful were allowed to wear the emblem. It was as if a new elite class of subjects was being created. A small, mercenary bodyguard also wearing the badge began to accompany the king wherever he went, eventually growing into something like a private army.

As Richard's ideas of himself grew in grandeur his manner became more lofty and god-like. At banquets in his newly rebuilt Westminster Hall he would sit silently at his raised throne in his royal regalia, watching everything but conversing with no one. If the king's eye caught someone, then they were required to bend one knee before him. In his desire to be venerated, Richard became increasingly aloof at court.

Then, in 1394, Richard's 28-year-old wife Anne died and everything changed.

They had married as teenagers and she was a source of calm in the king's chaotic life. There was genuine affection between the two. Royal marriages were foremost about strengthening alliances with other kingdoms, but Richard and Anne also loved each other.

Now Anne was dead and Richard beside himself with grief, as he showed at her funeral. The Earl of Arundel was late and Richard floored him with a hard punch to the face. Because this caused blood to be spilt on consecrated ground the funeral had to be halted while a purification ritual was performed. Arundel spent a week locked up in the Tower of London for his tardiness. Meanwhile, Richard ordered that the royal couple's Palace of Sheen should be torn down, despite it only being recently completed.

Despite these early warning signs of instability, Richard seemed to keep his kingship steady over the next few years: he led a successful invasion of Ireland in 1394, and in 1396 signed a peace treaty with France, even marrying Charles VI's seven-year-old daughter to cement the deal. But underneath Richard's increasingly cold exterior, a cauldron of rage was boiling.

In 1397, without warning, Richard launched a two-year reign of terror aimed, it seemed, at settling every grudge and grievance he had harboured since childhood. Richard had just turned 30 when the tyrant in him was unleashed.

The first of the Lords Appellant on Richard's list was the Earl of Warwick. The king invited him to a feast and afterwards had him arrested. Next, Richard rode with a host of his White Hart-wearing retainers to Pleshey Castle in Essex, the home of Thomas of Woodstock, the Duke of Gloucester. Woodstock,

Above: The White Hart became a sinister symbol adopted by Richard and worn as a badge by his private army.

THE DEATH OF GLOUCESTER

AFTER BEING ARRESTED, the Duke of Gloucester was imprisoned in a castle in Calais. Here, he did all he could to try and discover the seriousness of his situation. Gloucester was given his answer by his jailor in the following passage by medieval chronicler Jean Froissart:

"'My lord the King is a little displeased with you at the moment. He wishes you to stay here and put up with our company for a time. You will do that until I receive further instructions, which I hope will be soon."

…According to my information, just at the hour when the tables were laid for dinner in the castle of Calais and he was about to wash his hands, four men rushed out from a room and, twisting a towel round his neck, pulled so hard on the two ends that he staggered to the floor. There they finished strangling him, closed his eyes and carried him, now dead, to a bed on which they undressed his body. They placed him between two sheets, put a pillow under his head and covered him with fur mantles. Leaving the room, they went back

into the hall, ready primed with their story, and said this: that the Duke had had an apoplectic fit while he was washing his hands and had been carried to his bed with great difficulty. This version was given out in the castle and the town. Some believed it, but others not.

– THE CHRONICLES OF FROISSART

Above: The Duke of Gloucester is seized, arrested and taken to Calais.

Richard's uncle, was awoken in the dead of night by the king himself, and then thrown into jail. On hearing the news of Warwick and Gloucester, the Earl of Arundel simply surrendered to Richard. The charge against the three lords, Richard said, was treason. Gloucester, however, would not attend his trial: he had mysteriously died in captivity.

All of the Lords Appellant had now been punished except one: Henry Bolingbroke. The king's cousin was no safer than the king's uncle. Forced to swear loyalty or face exile or even death, Bolingbroke bowed before the king. It was a sensible choice: Richard quietly had Warwick exiled and Arundel beheaded. Revenge against the main Lords Appellant was complete. Chaos lay ahead.

Above: Richard II's coat of arms are shown on this stained-glass panel in St Mary's Church, Charlton-on-Otmoor, Oxfordshire.

THE TYRANT KING

Richard may have felt that by destroying the Lords Appellant he was seizing back control, but 'it was at this time that through the rashness, cunning and pride of the king, the entire kingdom was suddenly and unexpectedly thrown into confusion,' reported the chronicler Thomas Walsingham.

To settle the kingdom, Richard called a parliament on 17 September 1397. The packed hall was heavy with anticipation as Richard and his armed guard filed in. His personal bodyguard of 300 archers wearing the White Hart emblem spread out around the hall; a further retinue of soldiers surrounded the building. It was a clear statement of Richard's intent; for the rest of his reign he would rule as a tyrant, and his authority would be absolute.

As Richard sat silently on his raised throne, observing the room, his statement was read out to the parliament by the new chancellor, Bishop Stafford of Exeter: 'There shall be one king over them all. For the realm to be well governed, three things were needed: first the king should be powerful enough to govern; secondly, his laws should be properly executed; and thirdly, his subjects should be duly obedient.'

Therefore, the bishop continued, if the king were to be powerful enough to govern, he must be in full possession of 'his regalities, prerogatives and other rights,' and it was the duty of his subjects to report anything, or anyone, that would put these in jeopardy. To demonstrate his affection towards his realm, Richard would grant a pardon to all who had wronged him, 'except for fifty persons whom it would please the king to name'. Fear and intrigue rushed through the hall – who was on the list? Not one name, however, would ever be revealed.

Instead, Richard would invite anyone who felt they were guilty of a crime against him to seek a royal pardon. The 50, it was implied, already knew who they were. Now they could wipe the slate clean. Richard's ruse kept nobles in a constant state of terror and subjection. Over the following year, several hundred people stepped forward to ask for a pardon. All were punished severely. Richard did not reveal whether any of them were on his invisible list of 50.

Left: This 19th-century engraving shows the king arbitrating between Henry Bolingbroke and John of Gaunt during Act 1, Scene 1 of Shakespeare's *Richard II*.

With so many elusive traitors apparently evading justice, Richard was free to punish anyone in any way he saw fit. He confiscated lands, clapped nobles in irons and made new laws without parliament's approval. He extorted large sums from the shires accused of supporting the Lords Appellant and levied high taxes against the Church. Richard forced many nobles to put their seal to a blank piece of parchment. He could then fill it in with whatever he wanted – a letter of abdication, an agreement of a cash gift or a statement of treasonous intent.

In all of these actions, Richard felt the guiding hand of God upon him. In late 1397 he wrote a letter to the Count of Holland explaining that the punishment for crimes committed by traitors would also have to be borne by their offspring: as 'since the heinousness of their crimes demanded a heavier penalty that could be exacted upon their persons, we have, accordingly for a perpetual reproach to them, caused their punishment to be perpetuated upon their heirs, who must not climb to the pride of honours, but be forever shut off from reaching the height of any dignity or privilege.'

> WITH SO MANY ELUSIVE TRAITORS APPARENTLY EVADING JUSTICE, RICHARD WAS FREE TO PUNISH ANYONE IN ANY WAY HE SAW FIT.

This policy brought Richard into direct conflict with the one man he needed to avoid: Henry Bolingbroke. Since swearing his fealty to Richard, Bolingbroke had done everything he could to avoid irritating the king. His support had won him a new title, the Dukedom of Hereford, among the highest ranks of the English nobility. Another noble to retain the king's affection was the Duke of Norfolk, Thomas Mowbray.

Like Bolingbroke, Mowbray had been on the side of the Lords Appellant. Like any noble who had ever rebelled against the king, Mowbray now lived in constant fear of sudden, brutal reprisal. He called a secret meeting with Bolingbroke, itself a dangerous idea, and told the duke about a plot he had uncovered to take their lives. Richard's pardons were worthless, Mowbray said, and the king planned to kill both of them at the most opportune moment and then take their lands.

THE TRIAL BY BATTLE

THE TRIAL BY BATTLE of Thomas Mowbray and Henry Bolingbroke was held on 16 September 1398 in Coventry. The town was abuzz. Nobles and their retainers from across England had travelled to watch what was billed as the greatest duel of the age. Some in the crowd compared the spectacle to an Arthurian tournament; others could not resist being party to the latest instalment in the saga of their tyrannical king. There was an atmosphere of nervous expectation before the dukes took to the field.

Henry Bolingbroke arrived at 9 a.m. on a white charger decorated in blue and green. He proclaimed: 'I am Henry, Duke of Hereford, come to do my business against Thomas Mowbray, Duke of Norfolk, a false traitor to God and the king.' He was given some wine and took his place in his pavilion as his weapons were checked.

Mowbray himself then appeared, his horse decorated with red velvet and silver lions. He gave the same challenge as Bolingbroke, before riding to his own pavilion. Finally Richard himself arrived, to much fanfare. He was accompanied, as usual, by his royal bodyguard of 300 archers. Richard took his place at his pavilion and Mowbray and Bolingbroke mounted their horses and held their lances at the ready. The crowd fell silent as they waited for Richard's signal for battle to commence.

It did not come. Instead Richard called out for proceedings to be halted. He retired to his pavilion and the dukes did the same. After two hours, the Speaker of the House of Commons strode forward from Richard's pavilion to address the crowd. He announced the king had decided instead of bloodshed, he would exile Bolingbroke for 10 years and Mowbray for life. These sentences would have severe repercussions for both Bolingbroke and Richard. The crowd, however, simply went home disappointed.

Left: The trial by battle between Thomas Mowbray and Henry Bolingbroke was halted before a blow was struck.

The meeting put Bolingbroke in an invidious position. On the one hand, everything Mowbray had said could easily have been true and Bolingbroke should have been thankful for the warning. On the other hand, it could also have been a trap set by Richard to test Bolingbroke's loyalty; Bolingbroke would be committing treason if he did not report the conversation, and Mowbray, to the king.

Once again Bolingbroke did what he thought best for his own survival: he told on Mowbray. Richard swiftly had Mowbray arrested and jailed. Mowbray, however, vehemently denied the accusations against him. He insisted that no conversation with Bolingbroke had ever taken place. There were no witnesses to deny or confirm either man's account.

NOBLES AND THEIR RETAINERS FROM ACROSS ENGLAND HAD TRAVELLED TO WATCH WHAT WAS BILLED AS THE GREATEST DUEL OF THE AGE.

The dukes were then summoned before the parliament to present their arguments. However, both men remained resolute and nothing was solved. Richard then resorted to a judicial procedure that had been defunct since the early reign of Henry II: trial by battle. Mowbray and Bolingbroke would fight a duel to the death and God would confer his strength upon the innocent man.

After the cancelled trial by battle, Mowbray and Bolingbroke went into exile in France. Mowbray died soon afterwards of the plague. Bolingbroke himself was farewelled by a throng of followers lining the streets of London as he rode to the port. He would be back sooner than anyone expected.

On 3 February, 1399, John of Gaunt died. Duke of Lancaster and one of the most powerful men in England, Gaunt owned more than 30 castles and a vast swathe of land in the north. He was also Henry Bolingbroke's father and his death would provide the exiled duke with a great inheritance.

Bolingbroke, however, was in France and unable by law to return to England for another nine years. As he was therefore unable to claim his inheritance, Richard decided to claim it for him. He confiscated all of John of Gaunt's estates and extended Bolingbroke's exile for life. Now everything was clear: the duel

Above: Richard calls the trial by battle between Bolingbroke and Mowbray.

and the exile had merely been a means to an end; Richard had rid himself of the last of the Lords Appellant and made himself rich with the lands of Lancaster into the bargain. However, he had also sent a clear message to every landowner in Britain: your land is no longer protected by law, for I may take it whenever I choose. It was a fatal error. Richard's next mistake was to leave England open and vulnerable to invasion while he departed to put down a rebellion in Ireland. Waiting in France was Bolingbroke, Richard's new worst enemy. Now, with Richard gone, he swooped.

Bolingbroke sailed for England with a pitifully small force – only around 200 men. However, history had smiled on similar

efforts. Roger Mortimer and Isabella only had around 1500 men when they landed in England in 1326 to depose Edward II. When the couple landed, disaffected nobles flocked to join them; this is also what happened for Bolingbroke. Some chroniclers estimate that 100,000 English soldiers joined Bolingbroke, such was their hatred of Richard. The royal army summoned by the king's regent, Duke of York Edmund Langley, uncle to both Bolingbroke and Richard, similarly switched to Bolingbroke's side.

By the time Richard landed in Wales in July, Bolingbroke was in effect the new ruler of England. Richard disguised himself as a friar and rode to Conwy Castle with what was left of his royal bodyguard, for many of these paid mercenaries had abandoned him too. Richard flew into a rage at the news about Henry and swore that he would flay his cousin alive. Now, as his situation grew graver, Richard reportedly often burst into tears. Once inside the commanding fortress of Conwy, Richard called for aid from any noble still willing to come. None did. Richard's fate would now be decided by Bolingbroke.

A meeting between Richard and Bolingbroke, brokered by the Earl of Northumberland, took place at Flint Castle in northeast Wales. Northumberland had to coax Richard out from Conwy and rode with him, insisting that the meeting was simply to parley and agree the lawful return of Bolingbroke's lands. However, when the pair rode on to a hill overlooking the castle, Richard grew pale at the size of Bolingbroke's army. He demanded they return to Conwy, but Northumberland somehow convinced him to go on. 'Now I can see the end of my days coming,' Richard reportedly said.

Richard was given a last meal at Flint Castle while Bolingbroke waited for him outside. Bolingbroke's men told Richard's followers, 'Eat heartily and make good cheer, for by St George, your heads will soon be chopped off.' Bolingbroke, however, remained courteous and bowed before Richard as he approached.

> SOME CHRONICLERS ESTIMATE THAT 100,000 ENGLISH SOLDIERS JOINED BOLINGBROKE, SUCH WAS THEIR HATRED OF RICHARD.

Opposite: King Richard is shown setting out on his poorly timed invasion of Ireland.

Above: The meeting of cousins Henry Bolingbroke and Richard II at Flint Castle, Wales.

'My lord,' Bolingbroke said, 'I have come before you sent for me and I shall tell you why. I have come to help you to govern the kingdom of England, which you have not ruled well these 22 years that it has been in your government; and therefore, with the consent of the commons, I will help you govern it.'

In reply, Richard simply said: 'If it pleases you, fair cousin, it pleases us well.' Richard was then taken back to London as Bolingbroke's captive and imprisoned in the Tower. It must have been a poignant reminder of Richard's youth, when as a 14-year-old he and Bolingbroke had peered nervously at the rebellious peasants ransacking the city. Now the rebel was Bolingbroke and Richard's future had never looked so perilous.

After two weeks a small committee led by Bolingbroke visited Richard in the Tower. They were there, they explained, to hold Richard to his promise made at Flint Castle to abdicate the throne. Official reports say that Richard assented to this. Another eyewitness account describes Richard's reaction differently:

'The king was so enraged by this speech that he could scarcely speak, and paced twenty-three steps down the room without uttering a word; and presently he broke out thus: "You have acknowledged me as your king these twenty-two years, how dare you use me so cruelly? I say that you behave to me like false men, and like false traitors to their lord; and this I will prove, and fight four of the best of you, and this is my pledge."'

— *CHRONIQUE DE LA TRAHISON ET MORT DE RICHARD II*

Below: Richard rides into London as the prisoner of Henry Bolingbroke. He would be interned in the Tower where the two had taken refuge during the Peasants' Revolt.

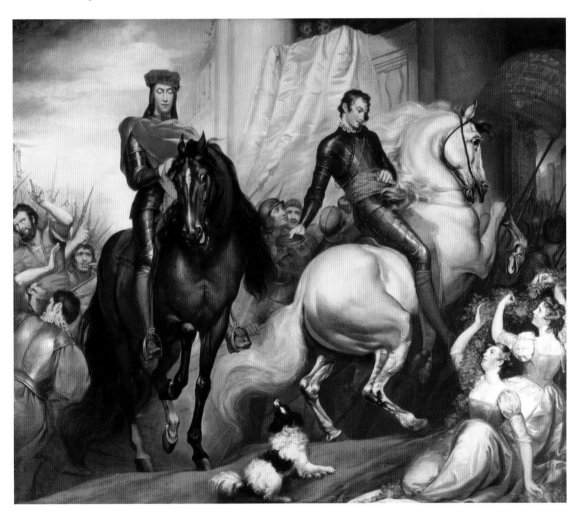

A Plantagenet king would never have quietly renounced his right to rule. But the decision was now out of his hands. On 30 September 1399, a parliament was assembled at Westminster to ask whether Henry Bolingbroke should be made the King of England. It was said that the cries of 'yes, yes' threatened to bring down the roof, such was Bolingbroke's support.

Bolingbroke was crowned on 1 October 1399. He would be the first king of the house of Lancaster and his claim to the throne was as a descendant of Edward III. Bolingbroke, now Henry IV, had Plantagenet blood in his veins, but he had set a dangerous precedent for the kingship.

Above: The 1399 parliament that assembled to depose King Richard II and crown Henry Bolingbroke in his place.

Despite everything he had done, Richard was still God's anointed ruler; he had been born into his kingship. Bolingbroke had snatched the crown through a coup d'état. Bolingbroke had broken the sacred rule of kingship; others with Plantagenet blood would now find it easy to do the same. From this point on, the house of Plantagenet would be irretrievably divided: Plantagenet would fight Plantagenet for the right to rule. The decades-long power struggle known as the Wars of the Roses would end in the complete destruction of the Plantagenet dynasty.

Richard II, the eighth Plantagenet king and the last to wear the crown legitimately, was under Henry IV's orders moved about to various castle dungeons in disguise before ending up at Pontefract Castle in Yorkshire. Here, he was denied food and water and left alone in a cell to die of thirst. His body was then dressed in black robes and taken on a tour of the country. This was done, it was said, so the dead king's subjects could mourn his passing; others conjectured that it was so everyone could be sure he was really dead.

Opposite: After King Richard's death in 1400, his body was taken on a tour of the country.

N ſtueran du
ſer cōmenr
par viīi xiī
deoy francie
iſſurēt de lee
logie et furēt trote battailles
de leure gēr. En la preme
re furēt ung huit cēe ba
ciners quattre mille archies
et quinze cēe arbaleſtriers

Et de ceſte auant garde fu
rēt cheſz le cōneſtable
les ducz dorleans et de bour
bon les cōtee du et de xi
eſchemont et pluſieurs aul
tre bone capitaīnes le cōte
de vendoſme et autree offi
ciere du roy furent ordōnez
a faire une elle a tout quīze
cēe hōmes darmes pour

7

HENRY IV & HENRY V

Henry IV would never live down his usurpation of the throne. He spent his reign searching for legitimacy while plots, uprisings and foreign invasion threatened. It was left to his son, the warrior king, Henry V, to restore honour to the Plantagenet crown.

R ICHARD II had been a hated king, but he had legally inherited the throne according to the Plantagenet rules of succession. He had also been anointed with holy oil as the sovereign of England under the gaze of God. Henry IV's greatest task was to prove to his subjects that he too, had a legitimate right to rule. To show his kingship had divine significance, Henry was crowned on St Edward's Day and anointed with holy oil that had once belonged to former Archbishop of Canterbury, Thomas Becket. The owner of the oil before Becket had supposedly been the Virgin Mary.

According to legend, Mary had appeared before Becket with the vial of oil, telling him that the first king to be anointed with it would be champion of the Church and recover all of the Plantagenet lands lost in France. Unfortunately for Henry, the effects of the oil were not beneficial. After being anointed,

Opposite: Henry V is commonly associated with his victory over the French at the Battle of Agincourt, shown here.

Above: The Virgin
Mary appears before the
Archbishop of Canterbury
Thomas Becket, bearing a
vial of holy anointing oil.

Henry's head became so infected with lice that his hair fell out and he was forced to wear a hat while it grew back.

It was a bad portent, but if divine aid was not forthcoming there was always brute force. This point was made at Henry's coronation banquet by Thomas Dymock, a knight who called himself the 'king's champion'. While the guests were being treated to a menu that included heron, eagle, bittern, curlew, crane, quail, egret, snipe, partridge, peewit, pullet and 'other small birds', Dymock leapt to his feet, drew his sword and made the following announcement: 'If there be anyone here, high or low, or whatever condition, who will say that Henry King of England, who is and hath this day been crowned, is not rightful king and rightfully crowned, as soon or on what day our lord the king shall appoint, I will prove with my body that he lieth falsely.'

While no one took up Dymock's challenge at the time, many considered Henry a usurper and even believed Richard II was still alive and in hiding. A group of these Ricardian loyalists mounted a rebellion against Henry at Windsor in 1400, but it was quickly put down. Needing to make an extreme example of anyone who disputed his right to the crown, Henry sentenced one of the rebels, Thomas Blount, to a public execution at Smithfield

Left: A 15th-century family portrait of King Henry IV with his wife and children.

in London. Here, Blount was placed on a stool before a fire with his hands tied. According to a contemporary account, the executioner soon arrived and begged Blount's forgiveness for having to oblige his office. The account continues:

'The executioner had with him a small basin and a razor, and kneeling between the fire and the lords, unbuttoned Sir Thomas Blount, and ripped open his stomach and tied the bowels with a piece of whipcord that the breath of the heart might not escape, and cast the bowels into the fire. As Sir Thomas was thus seated before the fire, his bowels burning before him, Sir Thomas Erpingham said, "Now go and seek a master who will cure you."…The executioner then asked him if he would drink. "No," he replied, "you have taken away wherein to put it, thank God!" and then he begged the executioner to deliver him from this world, for it did him harm to see the traitors. The executioner kneeled down, and, Sir Thomas having kissed him, the executioner cut off his head and quartered him; and he did the same to the other lords, and parboiled the quarters.'

— *CHRONIQUE DE LA TRAHISON ET MORT DE RICHARD DEUX*

Above: Rebellious Welsh leader Owain Glyndwr leads his army in battle against Henry.

Insurrection against the king did not only come from within Henry's own borders: Scotland and Wales both began raiding campaigns into England after he took the throne. There was also a running naval war with the French in the English Channel. To fight the Scots, Henry had enlisted the help of his main adviser, Henry Percy Earl of Northumberland. But after a time, Henry had stopped his financial support to help Percy keep the border safe.

Henry Percy and his son, known as 'Hotspur', travelled to London soon afterwards to confront Henry about money. The meeting ended badly when the king punched Hotspur in the face. Retaliation for this violence was to follow. Percy and Hotspur raised two separate armies against the king and then enlisted a further force led by the Welsh leader Owain Glyndwr. Glyndwr had led a popular insurrection against Henry IV from the time of his coronation and had captured large swathes of Welsh land previously under English control. To reward himself for this, Glyndwr had also started calling himself the Prince of Wales, a title that legally belonged to Henry IV's son, Henry of Monmouth.

In 1403, Hotspur raised an army in Chester and proclaimed he would dethrone Henry and replace him with Richard II, who he insisted was still alive. Waiting for his signal in Wales was Glyndwr at the head of another army, and Henry Percy in Northumberland with his own force. Before riding out to meet Hotspur at Berwick near Shrewsbury, the king took the precaution of dressing two of his followers in his armour; this, he hoped, would lessen the chances of assassination.

Henry wasted no time in riding out against Hotspur and had won the initiative: he engaged Hotspur's army before it could be reinforced by Glyndwr or Henry Percy. However, Hotspur had taken the superior position, with over 1000 archers lining up on a high ridge above the battlefield. The battle began two hours before sunset and was marked by the brutal efficiency of Hotspur's archers, who fired 'so thick and fast that it seemed to the beholders like a thick cloud'. Longbow archers proved at Berwick that they were the most formidable weapon in any army at that time: they could fire around 10 arrows a minute and carried two quivers with about 48 arrows each. This meant Hotspur was able to fire around 10,000 arrows a minute upon Henry's men: the result was great death and chaos on the battlefield, as the king's men were said to 'fall like apples in an autumn wind'.

As Henry's men began to fall back in great disorder, Hotspur launched a new attack. Spearheading this assault was Hotspur himself and around 100 knights whom he ordered to 'make an alley in the midst of the army' directly towards Henry. For a time, the impetus of this charge looked as though it would win the day, especially when the royal standard was captured.

Above: The Earl of Douglas and Hotspur are shown in the thick of the action together at the Battle of Shrewsbury.

All was confusion in the melee at the battlefield's centre when a cry went up that Henry IV had been killed. However, it was quickly revealed that the deceased was one of Henry's decoys and not the king himself. The Earl of Douglas, who was fighting with Hotspur, was heard to shout: 'Have I not slain two King Henries with my own hand? 'Tis an evil hour for us that a third yet lives to be our victor.'

The real Henry had been ushered off the field and the superior numbers of his army now surrounded Hotspur's knights. All was lost for the rebels when a lucky arrow caught Hotspur through his open helmet visor. Over 2000 of his men died with him as the royal soldiers took hold. It was said the field could not be seen through the bodies of the dead. The Wigmore chronicler called it 'a tragic and utterly lamentable battle in which father killed son and son killed father, kin slew kin, and neighbour slew neighbour.' The corpses were piled into a mass grave.

Below: Hotspur meets his end after being struck by an arrow through his visor at Shrewsbury.

Henry had quashed the insurrection, but it was only one of many to come. The next came from an unlikely source: the Church. In 1405, the Archbishop of York, Richard Scrope, enraged at new taxes Henry had levied against the Church, published a public list of grievances against the king. He then raised an army against him. The army was easily put down, but Henry's order that Scrope should be executed weighed heavily on the king. The execution had echoes of the murder of Thomas Becket and Henry began having violent, guilty nightmares. His health started to deteriorate.

ILLNESS AND END

Henry's nightmares began on the night of Scrope's death and they brought with them a mysterious illness that plagued him for the rest of his days. The symptoms included a burning sensation in his skin, and a disfiguring disease followed. It has been posited that Henry was suffering from leprosy, syphilis or maybe a form of psoriasis, but nobody knows for sure.

Whatever ailed Henry, he was in a weakened state when rumours reached his ears that his son, Henry of Monmouth, was planning to overthrow him. Henry of Monmouth was known to be one of England's best knights and had played a leading role in the king's victory over Hotspur. He joined the king's council in 1406 and had become a popular figure at court. As Henry began to withdraw from public life, Henry of Monmouth appeared to take control.

Suspecting a plot by his son, Henry confronted him at Westminster Hall. Here, Henry of Monmouth famously went down on one knee with a dagger in his hand, inviting his father

Above: Archbishop of York, Richard Scrope, is led to his execution after a failed insurrection against Henry IV.

to slay him if he wished, because 'my life is not so desirable to me that I would live one day that I should be to your displeasure'.

Whether this scene has been embellished or not, there was

a reconciliation between the two before the king's death on 20 March 1413. Given the severity of Henry IV's illness and the contents of his will it is hard to believe the king passed away peacefully. In his last document he describes himself as 'a sinful wretch' whose life had been 'misspent'. His body was entombed in Canterbury Cathedral, where it still lies today.

Above: Father and son are reconciled at this death-bed rendering of Henry IV's last hours.

HENRY V

Henry IV's usurpation and regicide of Richard II had hung over his entire reign. Many in England and abroad had never stopped questioning the legitimacy of Henry's kingship. His heir, Henry V, was determined to restore the reputation of the royal house of Lancaster. After his coronation in 1413, Henry decided to prove his right to rule through victory in war.

To many, Henry V seemed cast from the mould of the famous Plantagenet warrior kings who had preceded him. He was tall and lean with dark cropped hair and at 26 was an accomplished knight. Henry had fought Hotspur's rebellious army alongside his father at Berwick and nearly died on the battlefield. Henry was struck by an arrow below his eye that sank so far into his face that it became embedded in the back of his skull. Special tongs had to be made to extract the arrowhead, which lay stuck six inches deep. It took two months for the disfiguring wound to heal. Henry made sure his image was only ever shown in profile afterwards.

Opposite: A portrait of King Henry V. After the arrow wound picked up at the Battle of Shrewsbury, Henry insisted he was only painted in profile.

War was Henry's reason for being, but he was also a pious man who allegedly remained celibate until his wedding night.

He also showed he was willing to severely punish those considered heretics by the Church, even if they were his own peers. One such case concerned a knight named John Oldcastle, a childhood friend with whom Henry had fought alongside in Wales. Oldcastle was also a 'Lollard', a pre-Protestant Christian reform group founded by an Oxford seminary professor, John Wyclif. Wyclif had died in 1384, but his followers continued to be a thorn in the side of the church. Now, partly led by Oldcastle, the Lollards were gaining popularity once again. The Church looked to the new king to stamp them out.

In 1413, a proclamation was nailed to the door of a London church calling for all Lollards to rise up against their continued prosecution. A subsequent royal investigation led directly to a group of Lollards harboured by Oldcastle. Inflammatory Lollard literature was found among Oldcastle's personal effects and the knight was arrested. But, like many men held in the Tower of London, Oldcastle escaped. He then set about raising a Lollard army to kill Henry.

Below: Lollard leader John Oldcastle is shown during his execution by burning over a gallows.

In the event, the rebellion was as poorly conceived as it was executed. A small Lollard army gathered at London's St Giles's Fields under cover of night was quickly intercepted, captured and dispersed by Henry's men, who had been tipped off. Of those captured, 80 were found guilty of heresy and drawn from Newgate Prison and hanged along the highway leading out of London.

Oldcastle himself was not caught until 1417. He was taken to St Giles's Fields and hanged on a gallows above a fire that consumed both the structure and the man. As he burned he promised to rise again after three days, but his legacy as a proto-Protestant martyr did not blossom until the Reformation.

At that time, John Oldcastle was the original name Shakespeare used for his character Falstaff. Falstaff is the vain, decadent knight who appears principally in *Henry IV, Part 1* and *Part 2* as the hard-drinking companion of Prince Hal, the future Henry V. However, the bard was persuaded to change the name by Lord Cobham, a descendant of Oldcastle's, who felt his relation had been poorly represented in the play.

Meanwhile, Henry had shown he was both capable of stamping his authority on local rebellions and protecting the interests of the Church. He now turned his attention to that long-time obsession of Plantagenet kings: France.

The Plantagenet kings originally came from the French county of Anjou and from 1340 believed they had a legitimate right to France after Edward assumed the title of King of France. Now, Henry V sent word that he was making good on his great-grandfather's claim and borrowed heavily to raise an army. Notably, one of Henry's patrons was the wealthy London merchant Dick Whittington, who, according to his eponymous folktale, made his fortune by renting out his rat-catching cat to a faraway vermin-infested kingdom. It is not known if the real Whittington ever owned a cat.

TO MANY, HENRY V SEEMED CAST FROM THE MOULD OF THE FAMOUS PLANTAGENET WARRIOR KINGS WHO HAD PRECEDED HIM.

Below: Henry receives representatives from the Church during one of his parliaments.

CAMPAIGNS AND KINGDOMS

On 14 August 1415, Henry landed with his army on the French coast near the town of Harfleur. By doing so, the king was reopening the conflict now known as the Hundred Years' War; hostilities had ceased after Richard II's peace treaty of 1389. However, the Plantagenet blood in Henry's veins sprang from Anjou; now the king was back to reclaim his birthright.

Henry's force of around 6000 infantry and 2000 archers marched

directly to Harfleur and laid siege to the town. It lasted for less than a month and ended with the town's surrender. Most of the inhabitants were allowed to remain if they first swore their allegiance to Henry. A small English garrison was left at Harfleur, for Henry's aim was not just to take a town but the whole country.

Henry's next target was Calais, where he hoped to replenish supplies and rest his men. His besieging army had been camped out on wet marshland for too long, and many were suffering from fever as a result. Dysentery was also rife throughout the English ranks and malnourishment was common; there was simply not enough for the

Above: Henry instructs his men at the siege of Harfleur in France.

men to eat. Hundreds of men were lost to disease and many more were too sick to walk. Henry's ranks had been reinforced from England, but his weakened army still only stood at 8000 men. A torturous march to Calais now began.

Henry marched his army for about two weeks along the River Somme searching for a suitable place to cross. His army was shadowed by French scouts; the French army aimed to cut off the English and force a pitched battle near the village of Agincourt. As Henry's exhausted army approached, he grimly noted the superior French force 'swarming like locusts' around the village. The French army numbered somewhere between 20,000 and 36,000 men; the English were terribly outnumbered.

HENRY THE ORATOR

THE ODDS OF AN English victory at the Battle of Agincourt were stacked against Henry V. His inferior force was tired, hungry and sick. No army had ever been in such need of an inspirational leader. Luckily, this happened to be Henry V's speciality. He was said to possess great courage, energy and belief in his divine purpose. In this he resembled his predecessor, Henry II, being full of vigour and unable to sit still. Henry showed his skills as an orator after he and his generals saw the overwhelming size of the French army. The knight Walter Hungerford wished aloud that they had 10,000 more English archers at their disposal. But according to the anonymous text *Gesta Henrici Quinti* (The Deeds of Henry the Fifth), Henry bristled at Hungerford:

'To him the king said, "You are talking foolishly, because by the God of heaven, on whose grace I have depended, and in whom I have the firm hope of victory, I would not want to have even one more man than I have, even if I could. For these are the people of God I have here, and it is an honour for me to have them at this time. Or do you not believe," he said, "that his omnipotence, with these His humble few, can overcome the pride of the French that opposes him, who boast of their great number and strength?"'

— *GESTA HENRICI QUINTI*

It was stirring stuff, but threats and warnings also helped. Henry had told his men the night before battle that the French would remove the bow fingers of every English archer captured. He added that his men must remain silent on the night before battle, for risk of night-attacks, and that any who disobeyed would forfeit an ear.

Below: Henry performs the famous Agincourt speech later chronicled by Shakespeare.

On the morning of 25 October 1415, Henry ordered his men into position. They were placed, by the king's orders, on a narrow strip of field between two areas of forest. The thin English front line was flanked by two lines of archers on either side. Standing before them was the formidable French cavalry 'in a forest of lances and a grave multitude of gleaming shields'. Between the two armies was wet grassland made muddy by rain the night before.

For three hours the armies sat and watched each other without moving. Finally, fearing the French were holding out for reinforcements, Henry ordered his men to commence battle. The French plan was to use massed cavalry charges to mow down the English archers. However, Henry had learned of this strategy from a French soldier taken prisoner a few days earlier. To protect his archers, Henry ordered each to drive a sharpened stake into the earth in front of them. It was to prove a brutally effective tactic.

The knights on the French front line were said to be falling over each other to get at the English. They were organized into three facing lines. There were so many knights that the 4000 crossbowmen with them were not even deployed. The archers were told there was no room or reason for them. It was a costly mistake.

Above: An image of one of Henry's Agincourt archers protected by a stake against French cavalry charges.

Henry now ordered a volley from his archers, and a shower of arrows fell upon the French front line. This threw the French cavalry into disarray and a charge was quickly called. However, the horses were slow across the muddy terrain and then could not pass the stakes in the ground in front of the archers. Horse and man alike became impaled.

The French infantry was now ordered forward, but their progress was hindered by the increasingly boggy ground and the mass of arrows raining down on them. Bewildered, riderless horses also added to the confusion by galloping in all directions and trampling many French soldiers. A chaotic muddy melee now took place in the centre of the battlefield, according to the following report:

'Then a most bitter battle raged, and our [the English] archers notched the ends of their arrows and sent them against their flanks, continually renewing battle. When their arrows had been used up, they took up axes, stakes, swords and the heads of lances that lay between them, and laid the enemy low, ruining and transfixing them.'

– *GESTA HENRICI QUINTI*

Below: After exhausting their supply of arrows, the English archers picked up axes, swords and stakes and ran at the enemy.

The lightly armed English archers made brutal assailants as their armour did not bog them down, as it did the French soldiers. With a combination of heavily armed infantry and nimble archers, the English were able to destroy row after row of French soldiers marching towards them. Piles of French bodies were heaped everywhere and many trying to pass over them were simply crushed or suffocated to death:

'For *when some of them [the French] were killed as battle was joined, and had fallen at the front, the undisciplined violence and pressure of the crowd at the rear was so great that the living fell upon the dead, and even those falling upon the living were killed, such that, in the three places where there was a strong force and the line of our standards, the heap of those who had been killed and those who lay crushed between them grew so great that our men climbed the piles which had grown higher than a man's height, and slaughtered their adversaries at the rear with their swords, axes and other weapons.'*

Below: French and English cavalry clash in the muddy melee of Agincourt.

– *GESTA HENRICI QUINTI*

It was a rout, with two-thirds of the French army fleeing in terror. One of the most controversial elements of the battle arose when Henry was asked what to do with the hundreds of French knights taken prisoner. The murder of soldiers caught in battle was a terrible contravention of the medieval code of chivalry, but Henry panicked at a rumour that French reinforcements were close at hand.

He therefore ordered all the prisoners be killed by his archers and that any man who disobeyed him would be hanged. About 200 unarmed prisoners were slaughtered. In committing this atrocity Henry chose victory above honour. His victory, however, was emphatic: the English had lost 1000 men and the French over 12,000, including three dukes, 90 barons and 2000 knights.

CONQUEST AND CONTROL

After his victory at Agincourt, Henry V marched his army to Calais and then embarked for England. Here, he received a hero's welcome from over 20,000 Londoners at Blackheath. Henry's long-sought legitimacy as king was further bolstered by parliament's agreement to raise taxes to help pay for his war. From that point on, Henry IV's usurpation and regicide was not mentioned again.

Above: Henry V and Charles VI of France enter Paris together for the signing of the 1420 Treaty of Troyes.

But Henry had not finished with France. In 1417, he landed another army and began besieging one French town after another on his long march to Paris. He took with him the first cannon to be manufactured in Britain. The towns of Caen, Falaise and Rouen quickly fell before the now-feared English army. Within months, Henry was outside the gates of Paris demanding the crown of France be brought to him. It was an extraordinary scene with an even more extraordinary outcome.

The King of France was Charles VI, who during frequent bouts of madness would attack his own servants, run until he passed out or insist he could not be moved as he was made from glass. It was with Charles and his son the dauphin that Henry now hammered out the terms of a peace treaty; it took two months.

Under the 1420 Treaty of Troyes, Henry V would become the King of France upon Charles' death and in the meantime rule as regent. To cement this relationship, Henry married Catherine, the king's eldest daughter. Their son, Henry, was born on 6 December 1421. He would be the first king in history to automatically inherit the crowns of both England and France.

Below: Henry V meets his betrothed, Charles VI's daughter Catherine, at the French court.

It was an astonishing turn of events. Henry V had won more power and territory than any other Plantagenet king in history. But perhaps it was all too good to be true. There were already questions in the English parliament about the practicalities of the monarch also ruling France, and besides, not all of the territory there had been conquered. More violence would be necessary to confiscate the French land owned by the now disinherited dauphin. To add to all of this, the English clergy had stopped praying for Henry's successes in foreign wars.

Henry had come to the throne determined to secure his place as king through conquest: war was a great reconciler. But in the end, it seemed his achievements in the field had gone too far for his own people; there had been too much war. Neither would Henry die as a hero on the battlefield. Instead, like many other Plantagenet kings, Henry was fatally struck down by dysentery in 1422. So died the great model of the medieval king, a knight and conqueror in gleaming armour.

However, Henry V's legacy would not last: the French crown and the territories that he won would vanish almost as quickly as they had appeared. Today, it is Henry's famous victory at the Battle of Agincourt that is remembered as his single greatest achievement.

Above: Henry V's funeral. The king would not die on the battlefield but of dysentery, like many of his forebears.

Henry 6.th King of England & Fra[nce]

nd Lord of Ireland, *surnamed of Winds[or]*

8

HENRY VI

As the first Plantagenet to be crowned king of both England and France, Henry VI had a great inheritance to maintain. But as a ruler, he was weak-willed, indecisive and mentally unstable. His madness and misrule would plunge England into the devastating Wars of the Roses.

WITH THE DEATH of Henry V, there had perhaps never been such a strong need for a powerful Plantagenet king. Henry V had buried the spectre of Henry IV's usurpation, united the kingdom and extended its borders beyond what had been dreamed possible. But now this ungainly double-kingdom had to be managed with might and majesty, a task wholly beyond the powers of Henry VI.

The new king was only nine months old when he came to the throne, and so the kingdom was ruled on his behalf by his three uncles: Henry Beaufort, the Bishop of Winchester; and the dukes of Gloucester and Bedford. Like many other councillors who would dominate and control Henry, the three men bickered over most points of government and served only their own interests.

Opposite: A portrait of Henry VI in prayer. A pious, timid man, Henry was wholly unsuited to the throne.

By the time the eight-year-old Henry was anointed in Westminster Cathedral in 1429, Gloucester and Beaufort had already once raised armies against each other; Bedford had had to travel from France to bring peace. Control of France itself was already in disarray as the fight-back against English rule had begun under the unlikely leadership of a peasant girl, Joan of Arc.

Joan believed God had ordered her to lead an army against the English and install its previous heir, the dauphin, son of Charles VI, to the throne. With cropped hair and decked out in white armour, the 16-year-old Joan led an army of Charles VI's retainers to the English-occupied city of Orleans, where she won an unlikely victory and took back

Above: Joan of Arc leads her army into the English-held town of Orleans, France.

the town. Joan then marched alongside the dauphin to have him crowned King of France in Reims. This, in effect, would give France two kings: Charles VII and Henry VI.

Joan's luck was not to last and she was captured in 1430 during a battle near Compiègne. She then made a daring escape from captivity in Beaurevoir Castle by jumping 70m (230ft) from a turret into a dry moat; but she was recaptured and put on trial for heresy and witchcraft. The trial was a farce, which attempted to entrap Joan into professing her guilt; the only charge that would stick was that of cross-dressing. Joan was burned at the stake in Rouen town square on 30 May 1431. Afterwards, her body was burned twice more and the coals raked over so that nobody could say she had escaped from the embers.

Joan of Arc had begun the process that would win back France for the French under Charles VII although it would take 20 years. The blame for the mismanagement of England's rule in France was the bickering between Beaufort and Gloucester. However, there was also little stomach in the wider English parliament for the dynastic possession of France: why should English money be wasted on maintaining the continental kingdom? Especially, many argued, when there were so many problems at home.

The young Henry burst into tears when he heard about the repossession of Orleans: why, he wailed, had he been betrayed by his French allies, whom he had done 'no wrong to'? Such was

Above: Joan of Arc is burned at the stake after being accused of witchcraft and heresy.

the simplicity of Henry, who grew into a bookish, pious soul, timorous in manner but also generous where he could be. Henry would not conduct royal business on Sundays, disapproved of swearing at court, and freely scattered royal titles, despite the overabundance of nobles already in the realm.

While Gloucester and Beaufort argued about England's approach to defending Plantagenet lands in France, Henry busied himself with his pet building projects. These included Cambridge's King's College and Eton College, a school devoted to the education of those poorer subjects who would otherwise be denied one.

As this went on, Paris and parts of Normandy were falling to Charles VII. To take matters into his own hands, Henry held a secret meeting with Charles. Here a truce was struck between

Above: A Flemish portrait of the wedding between Henry VI and Margaret of Anjou.

the two kings and a marriage deal to settle it. In 1445, Henry married Charles VII's niece, Margaret of Anjou. The wedding at Westminster was a highly celebrated event: to Henry's English subjects it meant a pause in hostilities in France and promises of stability in England along with the prospect of a new heir to the throne.

Margaret's status would normally require a handsome dowry for the English coffers. Many were therefore horrified to learn that instead a dowry had gone the other way: Henry had gifted the French territories of Maine and Anjou to Charles VII as a wedding present. It was a seismic blunder and brought humiliation upon Henry's crown. No one imagined an English king would surrender land hard won through the lives of the nation's soldiers, especially not the beloved Plantagenet family county of Anjou.

Meanwhile, Henry's wife Margaret was showing that she too would dominate the king and undermine those in the king's immediate council. In 1447, Margaret had the Duke of Gloucester arrested on charges of treason and imprisoned. He died in sinister circumstances while awaiting his trial. Beaufort also died, apparently of suicide, in the same year. The old guard were out.

By 1449, the government was in a crisis. The English army in France was losing the fight to hold its territories after Charles VII broke the truce with Henry. The treasury's coffers were empty, and many harboured suspicions about the death of Gloucester. Into the void left by Gloucester stepped Richard Duke of York, himself a Plantagenet descended from the fifth son of Edward III; Henry was descended from the fourth son. York was therefore a potential claimant to the throne as well as being a powerful knight, and Henry did not trust him.

CADE'S REBELLION

JACK CADE WAS THE leader of a disaffected group from Kent who rose up against Henry VI in 1450 by marching on London. The group described themselves as 'petitioners' concerned at the country's 'lack of governance'. They wanted an end to corruption among Henry's advisers and a reversal of the losses of the royal lands in France. The rebel group included small landowners alongside peasants and English citizens recently expelled from Normandy by Charles VII.

This rebel army was around 5000 strong when it assembled on Blackheath and then attacked London on 3 July. Here, Cade cut the ropes on London Bridge, so it could not be raised to block the rebels off. He then proclaimed himself Mayor of London and set up a kangaroo court to try and execute those deemed guilty of corruption. The Lord High Treasurer and his son-in-law were beheaded on this charge, and their heads stuck on pikes and displayed on London Bridge, where they were positioned to look as if they were kissing.

Over the next few days the rebels fell to drinking and looting, alienating Londoners who had been sympathetic to their cause. On 8 July a battle broke out around London Bridge between the rebels and the king's army. Cade's men suffered heavy losses and disbanded. Cade himself fled to Lewes in Sussex, where he was captured and killed. His body was used for a mock trial as a warning against others. After being found guilty of treason, the body was dragged through London and then quartered, the pieces being sent to those towns believed still to be harbouring the other leaders of Cade's rebellion. The rebellion was temporary, but it showed the deeper and wider vexation of Henry's subjects.

JACK CADE *in* Cannon Street *declaring himself* LORD *of the* CITY *of* LONDON

Above: Rebel leader Jack Cade marches his riotous mob through the streets of London.

However, York's presence as one of Henry's advisers once again proved the king's inability to manage his own nobles. Partly as a result, discontent with the king was growing, and eventually led to the bloody conflict known as the Wars of the Roses.

The retaking of French territories by Charles VII took a little over a year. By 1450, only Gascony and Calais remained English; Henry had lost nearly everything for which his father had fought. The nobles now responsible for protecting the French lands – the Duke of York and the Duke of Somerset – blamed each other. They became sworn enemies from then on.

Henry's wife Margaret was often blamed and derided for the losses in France. The cost of the lost kingdom to Henry's credibility was far greater. But worse was to come: Henry had run the treasury dry: there was not enough money left to pay for England's administration. Moreover, the king was badly in debt and many rich merchants of London withdrew their support for him.

Below: Over time Margaret of Anjou showed herself to be the power behind Henry's throne.

In 1453 the court learned that Gascony had also been lost. Only a small enclave around Calais still belonged to England. This marked the end of the Hundred Years' War, which had started in 1337 under Edward II. The king had a complete mental breakdown. Coincidentally, days later Queen Margaret announced she was pregnant.

In October, Margaret gave birth to a male heir called Edward, and made him Regent of England during Henry's madness. Backing Margaret was the Duke of Somerset, but parliament demurred. The parliamentary members wanted their own man, Richard Duke of York, to be made Lord Protector while Henry was out of action, and this they did. Battle lines began to form behind York and Margaret.

THE WARS OF THE ROSES

The Wars of the Roses famously gets its name from the white rose sported by the Duke of York and his supporters, and the red rose worn by Henry VI and his Lancastrian supporters. Queen Margaret, however, was the real power behind the throne. Henry was so ill when parliament appointed York Protector that he hadn't even recognized his new son Edward.

Modern scholars have speculated that Henry inherited a type of schizophrenia from his grandfather, the French King Charles

Below: The Earl of Somerset is here challenged by the Duke of York. The supporters of Lancaster and York would thereafter wear red and white roses respectively.

VI, although the two had markedly different symptoms. Henry's illness was described by contemporary chroniclers as a type of catatonia: he sat for hours in a chair in a vegetative silence and could not rise or walk without help. Like Charles VI, Henry's illness would come and go for the rest of his life. However, the first bout of his affliction seemed to have something of a simplifying effect on the king's mind. His court was no longer surprised thereafter by odd quirks in his behaviour.

In 1455, Henry was well enough to be introduced to his son. His first order was to free the Duke of Somerset from the Tower of London, where he had been imprisoned by York on charges of treason relating to the loss of Normandy. Henry then set about reinstating other nobles ousted by York and called a parliament to be held in Leicester. York himself was not invited to attend. When this news reached York, he raised an army with the Earl of Warwick and marched to St Albans to intercept the king's party and demand his right to attend the parliament.

The Battle of St Albans is really only notable because it marked the first battle of the Wars of the Roses. In reality, the

Below: A map of the Battle of St Albans, a two-hour skirmish that took place in the streets of the town.

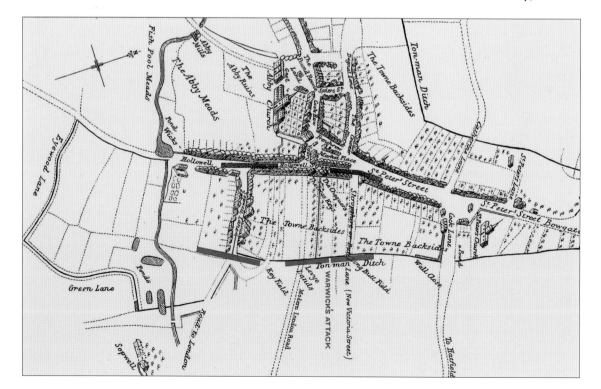

battle was a two-hour skirmish in the streets. It did, however, end in the murder of the Duke of Somerset, which had been York's main aim. York escorted Henry back to London. He resumed his role as Lord Protector a few months later when the king once again slipped into a catatonic state.

For the next five years, Henry fell in and out of illness and spent his moments of lucidity visiting abbeys and cathedrals around the midlands. Kenilworth Castle was the royal stronghold at this time, while York's powerbase was in London. Margaret continued to be the puppet master, and pulled every string to ensure the inheritance of her son Edward. Richard Duke of York's threat to the throne grew ever greater; he even started calling himself Richard Plantagenet, the first noble to do so.

In late 1459, on Margaret's orders, Henry called a parliament at Coventry and denounced York, Warwick and their supporters. The king also used the occasion to call all loyal nobles and their retainers to join a royal army. In reaction,

York and Warwick gathered their own army and marched towards Worcester. On 10 July 1460, the Battle of Northampton cost the lives of 2000 men. England fell into a savage civil war.

During the fighting at Northampton, Henry had been found by Warwick sitting quietly in his tent. He never fully recovered his faculties. York and Warwick escorted Henry to London and imprisoned him in the Tower. Here he was forced to sign a declaration that York, and not his son Edward, would succeed him as king. York's dynastic ambitions had been laid bare.

York, however, was killed at the Battle of Wakefield on 31 December 1460, his head cut off, fitted with a paper crown and placed on a gate overlooking the countryside. It was the only crown he would ever wear.

Above: The bloody Battle of Northampton tipped England into savage civil war.

Above: Margaret of Anjou places a paper crown on the severed head of the Duke of York.

The real king, Henry, was rescued after the Second Battle of St Albans on 17 February 1461. Margaret led the royal forces in this victory, and afterwards marched on London. However, Londoners would not lower London Bridge to let the queen into the city, such was the fear of her undisciplined army and its reputation for looting and murder.

Margaret had become a tyrant waging a war of terror against anyone opposed to Henry. Her network of spies and informers did not hesitate to use torture in interrogation, but none of this renewed people's respect for an ailing king. Henry had been seen laughing, singing and clapping his hands during the Second Battle of St Albans; to all those watching, the king was clearly mad.

Meanwhile, a new Duke of York, Edward, had replaced his fallen father. Edward was tall and confident and was reputedly one of the realm's greatest knights. As his father's son, he also

WARWICK THE KINGMAKER

BORN IN 1428, Richard Neville Earl of Warwick was a wealthy noble and formidable general. Warwick learned war as captain of Calais, a position that gave him control of all remaining English soldiers in France. On the battlefield, Warwick was the embodiment of the chivalrous 15th-century knight. He was a skilled and courageous soldier, who once, when all looked lost, slew his own horse to show his dedication to the fight. He would famously say at this moment: 'Let him flee that will, for surely I will tarry with him that will tarry with me.'

Off the battlefield, Warwick was a ruthless, self-serving opportunist. He was apt to change sides without warning if it served his interests; he seemed to care little for the general good of the English realm. His support for Edward Duke of York came at a crucial time in the Wars of the Roses, despite the lack of real trust between the two. Warwick also served Henry VI when it suited, and his role in the civil war earned him the deserved title of 'Kingmaker'.

Above: Richard Neville, 16th Earl of Warwick and 'Kingmaker'.

had a legitimate claim to the throne. Together with the Earl of Warwick, now the single most powerful noble in the country, Edward would change the dynastic fate of the Plantagenets.

THE BATTLE OF TOWTON

The Battle of Towton was the largest and bloodiest battle ever fought in England. Between 50,000 and 70,000 English soldiers met in one of the decisive massacres of the Wars of the Roses. The armies of York and Lancaster met on a swathe of frozen Yorkshire countryside on 29 March 1461. Soldiers from both sides were heavily armed with chain mail and plate armour and carried a lethal range of weapons, including swords, bows and arrows, clubs, poleaxes, battle hammers, maces, and spears.

At nine in the morning the battle began in the middle of a snowstorm, the howling wind combined with a whistling of arrows. Cannon fired thick pieces of iron and lead shot. The firing of missiles initially favoured the Yorkists, who had the wind behind them; many Lancastrian arrows fell short. To try to minimize the slaughter, the Lancastrians called a charge, sparking a brutal melee of hand-to-hand fighting; no quarter was given by either side. At first the Lancastrians had the advantage, and pushed the Yorkist line back metre by metre. But as the pushing and shoving went on, the front line swung around at a pivot. Now, the Lancastrians had the marshland today known as 'Bloody Meadow' at their backs.

Below: At the 1461 Battle of Towton, Yorkist archers with the wind at their backs inflicted terrible damage on the Lancastrian army.

Sensing their advantage, the Yorkists launched a cavalry charge to push Lancastrian soldiers into the marshland and the river running through it. The river quickly became piled with what one eyewitness called a 'bridge of bodies'; Lancastrian soldiers were forced to climb across the corpses to make their retreat. Many drowned. As Lancastrians fell over each other and became bogged down in the marshland they were brutally massacred by the Yorkists.

It was slaughter that seemed deeply personal in its barbarity: faces were split through the bone, heads and limbs repeatedly smashed, holes punched through foreheads with war hammers, and ears cut off as war trophies. Many Lancastrian soldiers threw off their armour and scrambled across Bloody Meadow and away. But they were chased down and killed, and no prisoners were taken. One eyewitness described bodies piled in trenches and pits as 'the blood of the slain ran down in furrows and ditches, along with melted snow in a most shocking manner.'

Below: At Towton, Englishmen slaughtered each other in snow, water and marshland.

There was a sickening
irony to the Battle of Towton.
Henry V had united the
soldiers of England to fight
the French using the same
methods of warfare that the
divided country now used
against its own. 'There was
the son against the father, the
brother against brother the
nephew against one nephew'
one chronicler reported. No
one was spared the horror
and butchery at Towton.
Over 28,000 were killed
during the rout by the Yorkist
army; the battle changed the
history of England.

Above: After Towton,
Henry VI escaped to
Scotland with Margaret
and his son Edward.

Henry VI, Margaret and their son Edward escaped by
riding to Scotland. Edward Duke of York rode to London with
Warwick, where he crowned himself Edward IV of England on
28 June 1461. With this, the Plantagenet line changed hands
from the House of Lancaster to the House of York.

Edward's coronation would not mark a clean-cut dynastic
change: Henry VI would have a last roll of the dice before the
end. However, Henry never recovered from his madness, nor the
dynastic ambitions imposed on him by his warmongering father.
Henry V had spent his reign trying to clear the family name after
the usurpation by his own father, Henry IV. Henry V's greatest
wish was that he and his heir, Henry VI, could rule without
shame over the vast kingdom he had created for them.

The legacy of the Lancastrians, however, was not to be one
of large, inherited kingdoms or a long-lasting dynastic line.
Instead, theirs had been a tale of usurpation: the taboo that
once broken could not be undone and instead had opened the
door for others to follow. The Plantagenet dynasty died in a
bloody welter of betrayal.

RICARDVS · III · ANG · REX ·

9

EDWARD IV, EDWARD V & RICHARD III

Edward IV was a handsome, magnanimous king whose coronation promised the return of a golden era to England. But Edward's weakness for women led to the infamous murder of his child heir and the rise of one of English history's most reviled villains: Richard III.

EDWARD IV appeared to be the king so badly needed after the bloodshed and turbulence of the Wars of the Roses. According to the chronicler Thomas More, Edward was 'a goodly personage, and very princely to behold: of heart, courageous; politic in counsel; in adversity nothing abashed; in prosperity, rather joyful than proud; in peace, just and merciful; in war, sharp and fierce; in the field, bold and hardy.'

Cheerful and approachable, Edward was a great diplomat who understood that to rule England well he needed a healthy treasury and the support of his barons. For much of Edward's reign, England prospered.

Opposite: A portrait of Richard III, one of England's most maligned monarchs.

Above: The coronation of Edward IV, the first Yorkist King of England.

Edward also strongly believed that the monarch should reflect the nation's wealth by his personal splendour. In the first year of his reign, the king spent the colossal sum of £5000 on clothes and jewellery for himself only. He owned hundreds of pairs of shoes, hats, furs and cloth of the finest golds, silvers, violets and crimsons. A bill from Edward's jeweller shows purchases of gold rings and crosses studded with pearls, rubies and diamonds; there is also a bill for a gold toothpick decorated with sapphires.

By appearance, Edward was tall, powerful and 'of visage lovely, of body mighty, strong, and clean made'. However, when of 'angry countenance he could appear very terrible to beholders'. Many women were greatly attracted to Edward and he had an insatiable desire for them. As a young bachelor king, Edward surrounded himself with a retinue of females and provided them with their own tents on hunting expeditions so he could visit them individually. Italian chronicler Dominic Mancini lived at Edward's court and reported the king to be 'licentious in the extreme'.

'It was said he had been most insolent to numerous women after he had seduced them,' Mancini continues, 'for, as soon he grew weary of dalliance, he gave up the ladies much against their will to other courtiers. He pursued with no discrimination the married and unmarried, the noble and lowly.'

Edward met his match in a woman of low birth he chanced upon while out riding in Northamptonshire. He was said to be instantly besotted with Elizabeth Woodville, once described as 'the most beautiful woman in the Island of Britain'. Woodville was that rare thing, a woman who would not submit to the king's advances. Nor would she agree to being just the king's mistress: if Edward wanted Woodville, he would have to marry her.

But Edward's marriage to Woodville sparked scandal, outrage and the beginning of the end of the Plantagenet dynasty. A royal wedding was foremost an alliance with a foreign power, a political arrangement traditionally discussed with barons and the parliament. Woodville was not a foreign princess with a powerful father and a handsome dowry: she was the English daughter of a knight and a widow with two children. Her father had even fought for the Lancastrian rather than the Yorkist side. None of these facts, however, deterred Edward. They were secretly married on 1 May 1464.

Below: A rendering of Edward IV courting Elizabeth Woodville. Their marriage would cause a royal scandal.

The marriage caused many divisions within the court, the royal family and parliament. Edward's mother, the Duchess of York, fell 'into such a frenzy' Mancini reported, 'that she offered to submit to a public enquiry and asserted that Edward was not the offspring of her husband but was conceived in adultery, and therefore in no wise worthy of the honour of kingship.' The king's younger brother, the Duke of Clarence, 'vented his wrath more conspicuously by his bitter and public denunciation of Elizabeth's obscure family.' A council of the king's lords told Edward that 'she [Woodville] was not his match, however good and however fair she might be, and he must know well that she was no wife for a prince such as himself; for she was not the daughter of a Duke or an Earl.'

Edward's greatest ally, Richard Neville, Earl of Warwick, was enraged by the news. Not only was the marriage a serious political miscalculation, but he, Warwick the Kingmaker, had not even been invited to the wedding. Warwick had spent many hours brokering a marriage between Edward and the sister-in-law of the French king, Louis XI. This negotiation had now ended in diplomatic disgrace.

Worse was to follow; Edward began bestowing land and titles upon the members of Woodville's immediate family. Woodville had five brothers and seven sisters, many of whom shared her famous beauty. The sisters were much desired by the nobles at Edward's court, even if marrying a parvenu diluted their rich blue blood.

It was not just the men who sought an attractive Woodville sibling. The new queen's 20-year-old brother was married off to the 65-year-old Duchess of Norfolk. The duchess, a wealthy widow of three deceased husbands, was also Warwick's aunt. Warwick was incensed at the union, which for him was the last straw. The kingmaker was to once again prove the truth of his title.

Above: A portrait of Elizabeth Woodville. The beauty of Woodville's seven sisters made them instantly popular at Edward's court.

It is an odd coincidence that around this time the ex-king Henry VI made an appearance. Last seen fleeing England after the Battle of Towton with his son Edward and wife Margaret, Henry had been living in exile in Scotland and the north of England with a handful of Lancastrian retainers. Henry still had support in the north, and was hidden by nobles there. Margaret had returned to her family estate in Anjou with Prince Edward, but her desire to put Henry back on the throne never abated.

Henry's luck, however, was about to run out. In 1465, he was betrayed by a monk while staying in Lancaster and then captured near the border. Henry had never regained his former state of mind. Although he had periods of lucidity he cut a sad and desolate figure. Wearing a simple straw hat, Henry was tied to his horse and taken to the Tower of London, where he was imprisoned. He spent five years there as prisoner 'Henry of

Windsor' so Lancastrian sympathizers would not try to break him out. When the breakout came it was after a Lancastrian insurrection against Edward, but thanks to one of Edward's most trusted allies: Warwick. Warwick had formed a rebel alliance with Edward's brother George, Duke of Clarence. George was the next in line to the throne if Edward died or was betrayed. The earl moved back to his estate at Warwick and refused all Edward's requests for an audience. Instead, Warwick began plotting with Edward's greatest enemy, Margaret of Anjou. By 1469, Warwick was in open rebellion against Edward IV. The embers of the Wars of the Roses had been rekindled.

THE READEPTION

Warwick made his first great strike against Edward IV at the 1469 Battle of Edgecote Moor, during which he took several high-profile prisoners, including Elizabeth Woodville's father and brother. Three days after the battle, on 29 July, Warwick captured Edward and imprisoned him in Warwick Castle. Warwick then called a parliament on the assumption that its members would call for Edward to be deposed in favour of his brother George. But Warwick was wrong. Parliament's loyalty still lay with Edward and they demanded his release. Warwick had little choice but to capitulate. Incredibly, Edward then forgave both Warwick and George.

Below: The Earl of Warwick here visits ex-king Henry VI in the Tower of London. Henry would spend five years imprisoned there.

Warwick hated Edward too much to give up the fight. He plotted with Margaret of Anjou for an invasion launched from France. In the meantime, he took advantage of Edward's absence in London to take control of the city and free Henry VI from the Tower. He then proclaimed Henry VI to be restored as king. Henry VI was crowned King of England, again, on 3 October 1470. On hearing the news, Edward fled in fear for his life to Burgundy. England once again had a Lancastrian king.

TO MANY THE CORONATION DID NOT SEEM REAL; IT WAS SIMPLY ANOTHER UNEASY EPISODE IN AN ALREADY OVERLONG SAGA.

This period is sometimes known as 'the Readeption [restoration] of Henry VI', but the king was only a puppet of Warwick and George. During his coronation, Henry had to be led by the hand through the crowds in London and said very little unless expressly prompted. To many the coronation did not seem real; it was simply another uneasy episode in an already overlong saga. Nor would Henry's readeption last. Less than a year later, Edward landed at Ravenspurn in Yorkshire with a small army. The army quickly grew to around 7000 men.

The armies of Warwick and Edward met at the Battle of Barnet, the decisive turning point in the conflict between the two. Warwick had tried to wait for the landing of Margaret of Anjou and her army, but bad weather delayed them. The armies clashed in a heavy fog on the morning of 14 April 1471.

Warwick's army heavily outnumbered Edward's by between 10,000 and 15,000. However, morale was low among Warwick's men and Warwick suggested he would fight on foot to rouse support. This was because mounted knights had a reputation for bolting when they began losing: Warwick would fight to the end.

The decisive factor in the battle was the fog, which did not lift. The Lancastrians easily outflanked the Yorkist line, but in the fog unwittingly attacked their own men. Cries of treason went up and a general panic ensued. Edward, quick to take advantage, ordered a charge into the centre of the field. As the fog finally started to lift, Warwick saw his brother being slain. Edward, also seeing this, called for Warwick to be spared: maybe through affection, or perhaps from a desire to have the earl publicly

executed. But it was too late; in the confusion the kingmaker
was killed. Warwick's body was displayed at St Paul's Cathedral
so that nobody could doubt his death.

Barnet signalled the end of the Lancastrian rebellion.
Margaret's army was annihilated after battling Edward at
Tewkesbury. Her son Prince Edward, died in the fighting and
she was jailed in the Tower. Here she stayed for four years until
Louis XI paid her ransom and she returned to France to live out
her days.

Henry VI was deposed and also imprisoned in the Tower,
dying on the evening of 21 May 1471. Edward, recrowned as
King of England the next morning, insisted Henry had died of
natural causes. However, when Henry's skull was unearthed in
our modern age, it was caved in and blood was still visible in its
light-coloured hair.

Above: Warwick the
Kingmaker is cut down
at the Battle of Barnet.
A stone obelisk was later
placed at the spot where
he died.

EDWARD V

For the next 12 years under Edward IV, England enjoyed a rare period of peace. The realm became prosperous as the wool trade flourished and a new merchant class was rising. William Caxton built Britain's first printing press, and ideas from the continent's Renaissance began to influence English culture.

Edward IV grew increasingly fat, using the peace to indulge his passions for food and sex. Elizabeth Woodville bore Edward 10 children during their marriage; countless other illegitimate children were also born. A king was expected to bed women other than his wife, and even to have a favourite mistress. However, heirs were only bred in wedlock. This legal point would soon assume great importance at the royal court.

Edward IV died quietly of 'natural causes' on 9 April 1483. The exact cause is unknown – it may have been a bout of pneumonia or typhoid; Edward was after all only 40. However, Edward had not died from murder, battle or dysentery, a rarity for a Plantagenet monarch.

Right: Anthony Woodville and William Caxton present England's first printed book to Edward IV.

Before he died, Edward had added a series of codicils to his will, sensing trouble brewing between his wife's family the Woodvilles and his brothers, George Duke of Clarence and Richard Duke of Gloucester. Edward had forgiven George for his treasonous support of Warwick, but George had later fallen out with Richard. Both men despised the Woodville influence at court, which had become more entrenched as the numerous siblings were married off to noble courtiers.

Isabel Dfs. of Clarence.   George Duke of Clarence.

Now, Edward's death set off a power struggle. Edward's heir was his 12-year-old son Edward, who was in Ludlow when he learned of his father's death. He was immediately acclaimed as the new king, Edward V. According to one of the codicils in Edward IV's will, Richard was appointed Lord Protector and Regent until Edward came of age. Richard now rode to collect Edward and bring him to London to be crowned. However, also riding to collect Edward was his uncle from his mother's side, Anthony Woodville, Earl Rivers. With him were 2000 retainers. Trouble was expected.

Above: George Duke of Clarence is shown alongside Lady Isabel Neville, the eldest daughter of the Earl of Warwick.

Both sides suspected the other would seize power through the boy king. By having Edward chaperoned to London at the head of a Woodville army, Elizabeth Woodville hoped Edward could then renounce Richard as Lord Protector. Thus the Woodvilles would be the power behind the throne. By letting Richard escort the new king, Woodville feared he would begin to dominate the boy and consolidate his own power. No one yet knew what Richard's plan was, except he did not intend to renounce his title of Lord Protector.

Richard and his 600 retainers met Rivers and the young king en route to London, alongside Rivers' 2000 retainers. Both parties greeted each other as friends and spent the night at Northampton together. But the next morning, Richard had Rivers arrested on a charge of treason. Rivers was then taken to Pontefract Castle and executed a few days later.

The next morning, Richard explained to his nephew Edward that Rivers had been the ringleader in a plot to depose him and had now been imprisoned. There were others involved in this plot, Richard continued, and 'these ministers should be utterly removed for the sake of his [Edward's] own security, lest he fall into the hands of desperate men, who from their previous licence would be ready to dare anything.' According to Dominic Mancini, Edward did not believe he was surrounded by traitors, saying: 'he merely had those ministers whom his father had given him; and, relying on his father's prudence, he believed that good and faithful ones had been given to him.'

Below: Elizabeth Woodville and her children seek sanctuary in Westminster Abbey after fleeing for their lives.

Back in London, Elizabeth Woodville and her family panicked at the news of Rivers' arrest. They believed it showed Richard wanted to kill them under the pretext of treason. Terrified, Woodville fled to Westminster Abbey to seek refuge with the Church.

Richard wrote to the mayor of London to insist he had no designs on the crown and instead wanted to deliver the king to London safely, for his own sake. This he did on 4 May 1483. On arrival, Edward was taken directly to the Tower of London in order to prepare for his coronation on 22 June. If Richard was going to supplant Edward, he had little time to organize it. But it was coming.

Elizabeth Woodville was still under the Church's protection at Westminster Abbey when news came that Richard was removing the Woodvilles from their positions in government. Parliament supported this; the nobles' long-felt resentment against the Woodville upstarts was surfacing. Richard granted many titles and gifts of land in return for the nobles' support.

news came that Richard was removing the Woodvilles from their positions in government. Parliament supported this; the nobles' long-felt resentment against the Woodville upstarts was surfacing. Richard granted many titles and gifts of land in return for the nobles' support.

Richard then wrote a letter asking royal allies to take up arms in the north 'to aid and assist us against the Queen, her blood adherents, and affinity, which have intended, and daily doeth intend, to murder and utterly destroy us.' One Woodville loyalist apparently intending to destroy Richard was the baron William Hastings. He was summarily seized and beheaded on a log of wood. It was a daring move: Hastings was a popular figure, but much more killing was to come.

On 22 June, the Church proclaimed that Edward IV's sons were bastards and not legitimate heirs allegedly because Edward had been betrothed to another woman at the time of his marriage to

Above: Heir apparent Edward V rides into London accompanied by his uncle Richard, Duke of Gloucester.

Elizabeth Woodville and therefore their wedding was fraudulent. This made Richard the rightful heir to the throne of England. On 6 July, he was crowned King Richard III.

The purge of his enemies, the seizure of power and the delegitimizing of the Woodvilles were shocking in themselves, but other Plantagenets had done far worse. Then came news of an unprecedented atrocity. Edward V and his brother Richard, who had been keeping him company, had both disappeared from the Tower of London. They were never seen again.

History has assumed that Richard was responsible for the murder of the nephews in the Tower, for there can be few other reasonable explanations for their disappearance. The crime, immortalized by Shakespeare, has made Richard III the most maligned of all the Plantagenet kings, if not of all British monarchs. Richard, of course, had not been the first to kill an imprisoned nephew. King John had also had his nephew Arthur murdered when his crown was threatened.

Perhaps by 1483, people were more enlightened: the murder of two innocent boys was seen as a crime against God and the natural order. But there was no evidence to link the murder with Richard, nor has any been found since. The mystery of the 'Princes in the Tower' certainly remained unsolved during Richard's time, but it did have the effect of bringing about his own demise.

RICHARD THE MAN

THOMAS MORE WAS A medieval lawyer, MP and saint who wrote a 16th-century chronicle about Richard III. His description of the king follows:

'Richard, the third son, of whom we now treat, was in wit and courage equal with either of them, in body and prowess far under them both: little of stature, ill featured of limbs, crooked-backed, his left shoulder much higher than his right, hard-favoured in appearance, and such as is in the case of lords called warlike, in other men called otherwise. He was malicious, wrathful, envious, and from before his birth, ever perverse. It is for truth reported that the Duchess his mother had so much ado in her travail to birth him that she could not be delivered of him uncut, and he came into the world with the feet forward, as men be borne outward, and (as the story runs) also not untoothed...

He was close and secret, a deep dissembler, lowly of countenance, arrogant of heart, outwardly friendly where he inwardly hated, not omitting to kiss whom he thought to kill; pitiless and cruel, not for evil will always, but for ambition, and either for the surety or increase of his estate. Friend and foe was much the same; where his advantage grew, he spared no man death whose life withstood his purpose.'

– THE HISTORY OF KING RICHARD THE THIRD, THOMAS MORE

Above: A portrait of the king as imagined from Shakespeare's Richard III.

THE BATTLE OF BOSWORTH

Richard III's reign brought an ignominious end to the Plantagenet dynasty, the longest in English history. On the other hand, like a true Plantagenet king, Richard did not give up his life or his crown easily. Maligned as a monster and murderer, still the king went down in a blaze of sword blades, like a brave if black knight from the annals of King Arthur.

The end came at the storied Battle of Bosworth, where Henry Tudor, the new head of the House of Lancaster, returned from self-exile in France at the head of an invading army. Tudor was another who thought he had a fair claim to the English throne, through his mother Margaret Beaufort, great-granddaughter of John of Gaunt, the son of Edward III.

Tudor was raised by his uncle, Jasper, who fled to Brittany after the Lancastrian defeat at the 1471 Battle of Tewkesbury. As an exiled Lancastrian noble living in France, Tudor had been waiting for an opportunity to return to England and reclaim, at the very least, his lands, and with luck, the crown. Tudor intended to marry Elizabeth of York upon his return, an alliance that would bring together the two houses responsible for the Wars of the Roses.

Below: A plaque commemorating the landing of Henry Tudor in Wales at the head of an army.

In August 1485, Henry Tudor landed with a small force in Wales, and then marched 200 miles to meet Richard in battle. Tudor's army grew to around 5000 men by the time he arrived at Bosworth, a marshy field in Leicestershire. Richard's army, by comparison, was three times the size at 15,000 men. However, the key difference between the two was motivation. Tudor's men were keen to give battle, whereas the allegiance of Richard's allies was shaky and uncertain.

The battle began with cannon fire and volleys of arrows. The first primitive handguns also made an appearance at Bosworth, alongside small daggers, halberds and battleaxes. Maces were favoured by fighting members of the clergy, who by clerical law were not allowed to draw blood, but could instead smash the bones of their opponents.

After some initial missile fire, Richard ordered his men to charge and the usual melee began. Of the few contemporary

Below: Richard III here meets his end after fighting valiantly at the 1485 Battle of Bosworth.

accounts of the battle, all praise Richard for his bravery. Despite being short and crooked, Richard reportedly killed the tallest Lancastrian knight on the field that day, the 2m-tall (6ft 8in) John Cheyney. He also killed Tudor's standard bearer. Richard's own standard bearer, by comparison, had both his legs cut from under him, but kept the royal colours raised.

Richard's determination, however, was not matched by many of his soldiers. One of his commanders, Thomas Stanley, was notably hanging back from battle and refused to give the order for his 6000 men to engage. Richard sent word that he would kill Stanley's son if he did not start fighting. Stanley sent word back that he had other sons. This news seemed to presage disaster for Richard; some of his men had already begun fleeing the battlefield.

SEEING HE WAS BETRAYED, RICHARD BELLOWED 'TREASON! TREASON!' AS STANLEY'S MEN BORE DOWN ON HIM.

It was at this time that one of Richard's bodyguard asked if he wanted a horse to beat a retreat. 'God forbid I yield one step,' Richard is reported to have said, placing his crown on his head. 'This day I will die as a king or win.'

To this end, Richard led a death-or-glory charge at Henry himself, isolated on a nearby hilltop with a handful of retainers. The unwritten rule of medieval warfare was that an army would stop fighting if its commander was killed: Richard had decided to chop the head off of the snake.

Seeing Richard's charge, Stanley finally ordered his men into battle, but on the side of Henry. Seeing he was betrayed, Richard bellowed 'Treason! Treason!' as Stanley's men bore down on him. Richard was said to have fought to the last. The medieval historian John Rous, who once called Richard the 'Antichrist', praised his valour at Bosworth: 'If I may say the truth to his credit, though small in body and feeble of limb, he bore himself like a gallant knight and acted with distinction as his own champion until his last breath.'

Surrounded and battered, his skull sliced open, Richard fell headlong into a brook (later deemed taboo to drink). The king's body was stripped naked, thrown over a horse and paraded past Henry's men, who had now won the day. Richard's crown

was found lying on the battlefield and taken to be placed on Henry's head. The last Plantagenet king was dead; the reign of the Tudors had begun.

Richard's body was discovered over 500 years later, crammed into a clumsily dug grave beneath a car park in Leicester. The skeleton showed Richard to be a small man, only 1.72m (5ft 8in) tall, with an unusually slender, almost feminine build. Richard's last moments had been savage: eight blows to the head, one of which slashed away an entire flap of bone from his skull and made a cut through to the other side – a wound of more than 10cm (4in). Other wounds indicate slashes to the face and an upthrust through the buttocks – the ritual injuries of humiliation committed after death against a hated foe.

Following his death at Bosworth, Richard became the only Plantagenet king not to be buried in a church. His remains were at last transferred to holy ground in 2013, at Leicester Cathedral. The Plantagenet king had finally been laid to rest.

Opposite: Henry is crowned at Bosworth following Richard's demise. The king is dead, long live the king.

Below: The funeral of Richard III took place after his skeleton was found buried beneath a car park in 2013.

CONCLUSION

The accession of Henry Tudor to the throne marked the end of the Plantagenets and the English Middle Ages. The Plantagenet dynasty had been forged in the violence of bloody civil war; now it was destroyed in the same way. The family line ended in oblivion.

THE STORY of the Plantagenets had always been about family politics. At its heart lay the fundamental question: who should be king? The answer was seldom clear-cut. The pattern of succession from father to eldest son was constantly interrupted by armed conflict. During 331 years of Plantagenet rule, war frequently erupted between members of the same dynasty: sons attacked fathers, brothers attacked brothers, uncles attacked nephews; internecine violence was a Plantagenet institution.

As with most other families, the great turning points in the Plantagenet story came with deaths, births and marriages. It was of paramount importance to provide at least one male heir and preferably more to ensure the royal line. These sons were expected to be strong, military-minded and fearsome generals on the battlefield. To command respect in the Middle Ages, kings above all had to be warriors. Richard the Lionheart, a sovereign who cared little for England or his subjects, is still

Opposite: Richard the Lionheart was fond of recounting the legend behind his supposed demonic lineage, saying 'From the devil we sprang and to the devil we shall go'.

venerated as the nation's crusading strongman; Edward II is reviled as an effete weakling.

Edward II is chiefly remembered not for his reign but the bad company he kept. His obsession with Piers Gaveston and then Henry Despenser brought about his alleged murder by hot poker; such is the lurid brutality of the line. Edward, however, was not the only Plantagenet who was a poor judge of character: Henry III was nearly destroyed by his one-time best friend Simon de Montfort and Henry II felt forced to kill his former favourite, the archbishop, Thomas Becket.

Above: Henry III's barons forced parliamentary reforms upon him, despite his best efforts to resist them. The reforms, however, had little to do with democratic ideology.

The king's relationship with his court was always central. Often the new Plantagenet ruler was still a child and at the mercy of a council of nobles who governed the kingdom and 'guided' the unready monarch. Few nobles lacked an agenda. Those kings who survived the transition into adult power were often either incompetent or dangerous. Richard II launched a reign of terror as soon as he could depose his royal council; Henry VI gave away half his kingdom before suffering a nervous breakdown.

What did these kings think of their royal position? Some genuinely believed in their divine right to rule; others had at least been told so from birth. But the search for support from powerful others suggests insecurity rather than mere narcissism. The king always needed to come to an arrangement with his rivals and enemies. It is easy to condemn Plantagenet stupidity and self-indulgence. But Edward IV, for instance, clearly understood that a successful reign meant keeping the royal coffers full and the barons on side. It was difficult to do both, because excessive royal taxes could spark a barons' revolt. Plantagenet kings were born into a constant power struggle.

It is even possible to feel some empathy for the Plantagenets and the dilemmas they faced. But empathy is harder when you consider the lives of ordinary Englanders. Life for them was generally harsh, brutal and short; most people lived in places that moderns would find wretched, squalid and dangerous; many died horrible deaths following crop failure or untreatable sickness. And always they had to be ready to fight for their baron or their king. They received little in return.

It was not for the ordinary English people that parliament and law courts were introduced: they were devices to increase royal revenue, or to reduce the power of the Church, or to tilt the balance of power between the barons and king. However, these institutions, which today form the basis of democratic government, are often considered the Plantagenets' greatest legacy.

The Plantagenets themselves usually resisted all reforms that impinged on their royal power. John manoeuvred to avoid the restrictions of Magna Carta and Henry III asked the pope to help him renege on the Provisions of Oxford. Simon de Montfort jailed Henry for his betrayal of the Provisions; later, when the king fought back, he was executed and his testicles hung from his nose. Little quarter was given in this perennial power struggle. However, the Provisions would help pave the way for an elected House of Commons. The introduction of a constitutional monarchy would later follow.

However, this upper-level power struggle had little bearing on most people's lives. Only in the Peasants' Revolt of 1381 did a sudden change to their subjection under the feudal system seem possible. But this hope

Below: For a short period during the 1381 Peasants' Revolt, it seemed as if the feudal system could be overthrown.

The Burning of St. John's Monastery near Smithfield, by Wat Tyler's Mob, in the Reign of Richard II.

was extinguished in a savage betrayal and brutal round of beheadings by Richard II.

For most people, life moved slowly and according to the rhythms of the countryside; their chief concerns were seasons, harvests and weather. What did the lives of the Plantagenet kings mean to them? They must have been of limited or sporadic interest, aside from the pleasure of gossip. Magna Carta didn't change the lives of the peasants.

England was already an old country by the time the Plantagenets arrived and its people were made up of the many different nationalities who had invaded and settled there: the Celts, Romans, Vikings, Anglo-Saxons and Normans. England's later kings would be Scottish, Dutch and German. Like the

Below: Edward III created the Order of the Garter as a chivalrous honour bestowed upon valiant knights for battlefield bravery.

Plantagenets, some of these new rulers had little knowledge of English when they arrived, but over time they helped England create its national identity. England, after all, is a repeatedly colonized and hybrid nation.

The first generation of Plantagenet kings did not consider themselves even vaguely English when they took the throne. French was the language of the court, and English spoken by the peasantry. However, after John lost the Plantagenet territories in France this slowly began to change. Edward III made English the official language of government and considered England a nation rather than a Plantagenet possession. Edward confirmed the country's national symbols by marching armies under the banner of St George, and by founding that most aristocratic English institution, the Order of the Garter.

Edward built Windsor Castle as his Camelot, just as Henry III built Westminster Abbey in memory of Edward the Confessor, the Anglo-Saxon king so admired by the Plantagenets. Churches and cathedrals are the physical testament of Plantagenet rule. But like their roads and villages, these were always built over the ancient trackways and foundations laid long before, some down to the roots of the country's Neolithic past.

However, building works, parliaments and law courts is not why we remember the Plantagenets. Instead it is the murder and betrayal, the scandals and cruelty, the gilded squalor and the blood-stained glamour.

Below: The mystery of the 'Princes in the Tower' remained unsolved during Richard's time, but it did help bring about the king's demise.

BIBLIOGRAPHY

Ackroyd, Peter, *Foundation: A History of England Volume I* (Macmillan, 2011)

Allmand, C, *The Hundred Years War: England and France at War c.1300–c.1450* (Cambridge University Press, 2008)

Barber, R. & Barber, J., *Tournaments: Jousts, Chivalry and Pageants in the Middle Ages* (Boydell Press, 2013)

Bartlett, Robert, *England under the Norman and Angevin Kings: 1075–1225* (Oxford University Press, 2000)

Brundage, J. A., *Richard Lionheart* (Scribners, 1974)

Carpenter, D. A, *The Minority of Henry III* (University of California Press, 1992)

Clanchy, M. T., *England and its Rulers: 1066–1307* (Wiley–Blackwell, 2014))

Desmond, Seward, *The Demon's Brood: A History of the Plantagenet Dynasty* (Pegasus, 2017)

Flori, Jean, *Richard the Lionheart: King and Knight* (Edinburgh University Press, 2006)

Froissart, Jean, *Chronicles* (Penguin Classics, 1978)

Gillingham, John, *The Wars of the Roses* (Weidenfeld & Nicolson, 1981)

Goodman, Anthony, *The Wars of the Roses: Military Activity and English Society, 1452–97* (Routledge, 1990)

Haines, R. M., *King Edward II: His Life, His Reign, and Its Aftermath, 1284–1330* (McGill–Queen's University Press, 2006)

Hallam, E. M. (ed.), *The Plantagenet Chronicles: Medieval Europe's Most Tempestuous Family* (Tiger Books, 1996)

Hamilton, J. S., *The Plantagenets: History of a Dynasty* (Continuum, 2013)

Harding, Alan, *England in the Thirteenth Century* (Cambridge University Press, 1993)

Harriss, G. L., *Shaping the Nation: England 1360–1461* (Oxford University Press, 2005)

Harvey, John, *The Plantagenets* (Collins, 1959)

Hicks, Michael, *The Wars of the Roses* (Yale University Press, 2012)

Hollister, C. Warren, *Henry I* (Yale University Press, 2001)

Horrox, Rosemary (ed.), *The Black Death* (Manchester University Press, 1994)

Jones, Dan, *The Plantagenets* (William Collins, 2013)

Keen, Maurice, *Chivalry* (Yale University Press, 2005)

Loach, Jennifer, *Edward VI* (Yale University Press, 2002)

Maddicott, J. R., *Simon de Montfort* (Cambridge University Press, 1996)

Morris, Marc, *King John: Treachery, Tyranny and the Road to Magna Carta* (Windmill Books, 2016)

Mortimer, Ian, *The Perfect King: The Life of Edward III, Father of the English Nation* (Vintage, 2008)

Ormrod, W. M., *The Reign of Edward III* (The History Press, 2000)

Phillips, Seymour, *Edward II* (Yale University Press, 2011)

Powicke, F. M., *Medieval England 1066–1485* (Oxford University Press, 1942)

Prestwich, Michael, *Plantagenet England: 1225–1360* (Oxford University Press, 2005)

Rogers, C. (ed.) *The Wars of Edward III: Sources and Interpretations* (Boydell Press, 2010)

Ross, Charles, *Richard III* (Yale University Press, 1999)

Saul, Nigel, *For Honour and Fame: Chivalry in England, 1066–1500* (Pimlico, 2012)

Stones, E. L. G., *Edward I* (Oxford University Press, 1968)

Sumption, Jonathan, *Trial by Battle: The Hundred Years War, Vol. 1 & 2* (Faber & Faber, 1999)

Tuck, A., *Richard II and the English Nobility* (Edward Arnold, 1973)

Turner, R. V., *The Reign of Richard Lionheart: Ruler of the Angevin Empire, 1189–1199* (Routledge, 2000)

Warren, W. L., *Henry II* (Yale University Press, 2000)

Wilson, Derek, *The Plantagenets* (Quercus, 2011)

Wolffe, Bertram, *Henry VI* (Yale University Press, 2000)

Waugh, S., *England in the Reign of Edward III* (Cambridge University Press, 2010)

INDEX

PICTURE CREDITS

Alamy: 8 top (Timewatch Images), 11 (De Luan), 17 (F8 Archive), 18 (2d Alan King), 19 (North Wind Picture Archive), 20 (Walker Art Library), 21 (Chris Poole), 24 (Lebrecht Music & Arts), 25 (Hirarchivum Press), 26 (Timewatch Images), 27 (Peter J Hatcher), 33 (Print Collector), 42 (Paul Fearn), 43 (2d Alan King), 46 (Art Collection 2), 49 (Walker Art Library), 52 (Archivart), 56 (Josse Christophel), 57 (19th Era), 58 (G L Archive), 59 (Hemis/Maisant Ludovic), 62 (Colin Underhill), 66 (Art Directors & TRIP/Helene Rogers), 67 (Timewatch Images), 74 (Everett Collection), 78 (Lebrecht Music & Arts), 79 (Falkensteinphoto), 80 (Timewatch Images), 84 (Lordprice Collection), 91 top (Lebrecht Music & Arts), 95 (Timewatch Images), 96 (Robert Herrett), 100 & 102 (Artokoloro Quint & Lox), 105 (North Wind Picture Archive), 112 (Niday Picture Library), 118 (Glasshouse Images/J T Vintage), 120 (19th Era), 121 (ART Collection), 123 (Niday Picture Library), 127 (Interfoto), 230 (Pictorial Press), 138 (Artokoloro Quint & Lox), 142 (ART Collection), 143 (Ian Dagnall Computing), 145 (De Luan), 147 (2d Alan King), 148 (Colin Underhill), 164 (Lordprice Collection), 172 (Artokoloro Quint & Lox), 179 (Yolanda Perera Sanchez), 182 (Historical Image Collection by Bildagentur-online), 186 (Florilegus), 188 (Paul Fearn), 189 (2d Alan King), 192 (G L Archive), 194 (Stocktrek Images/John Parrot), 199 (19th Era), 201 (Lebrecht Music & Arts), 204 (19th Era), 207 (Camera Lucida), 210 (G L Archive), 214 (Walker Art Gallery), 216 (Art Collection)

Alamy/Chronicle: 9, 23, 32, 40, 44, 65, 73, 98, 103, 107, 119, 126, 131, 135, 144, 154, 159, 162, 173, 177, 178, 180, 185, 190 top, 196, 203, 205, 208, 215

Alamy/Classic Image: 48, 55, 69, 89, 97 top, 124, 153, 156, 190 bottom

Alamy/Granger Collection: 12, 30, 36, 87, 91 bottom, 114, 116, 125, 132, 149, 169, 184, 206

Alamy/Heritage Images Partnership: 8 bottom (Historica Graphica Collection), 16 (Museum of London), 50 (Fine Art Images), 51 (Print Collector), 64 (Print Collector), 68 (Fine Art Images), 83 (Historica Graphica Collection), 128 (Fine Art Images), 134 (Historica Graphica Collection), 141 (Historica Graphica Collection), 146 (Fine Art Images), 193 (Guildhall Library & Art Gallery)

Alamy/Historical Images Archive: 31, 35, 53, 70, 76, 82, 93, 110, 151, 158, 165, 167, 175

Alamy/World History Archive: 88, 113, 137, 163, 166, 168, 170, 183, 191, 202

Amber Books: 174

Bridgeman Images: 157 (Royal Albert Memorial Museum), 187 (Houses of Parliament)

Depositphotos: 92 (Nora Bana), 97 bottom (Georgios)

Dreamstime: 61 (Roy Pederson), 81 (David Martyn), 94 (Sebastian423)

Getty Images: 14 (Universal History Archive), 28 & 29 (Universal Images Group), 47 (Corbis/Leemage), 72 (De Agostini/Dagli Orti), 86 & 108 (Time Life Pictures), 136 (Print Collector), 211 (Christopher Furlong), 212 (Art Images), 217 (De Agostini/Dagli Orti)

Getty Images/Hulton: 6 (Print Collector), 10 top, 99 (Print Collector), 117, 139, 160 (Heritage Images), 171 & 176 (Print Collector), 197 (Heritage Images), 198 (Print Collector)

Public Domain: 60

Shutterstock: 10 bottom (Filip Fuxa), 15 (Flik47), 37 (Mountainpix), 38 (Alex Yeung), 90 (Peresanz), 106 (Ulmus Media)